The Art of Bible Journaling

The
HOLY BIBLE

The Art of Bible Journaling

More than 60 Step-by-Step Techniques for Expressing Your Faith Creatively

Erin Bassett

 Get Creative 6

Get Creative 6

An imprint of Mixed Media Resources

104 West 27th Street

New York, NY 10001

Editorial Director
JOAN KRELLENSTEIN

Senior Editor
MICHELLE BREDESON

Art Director
IRENE LEDWITH

Managing Editor
LAURA COOKE

Associate Editor
JACOB SEIFERT

Still-life Photography
MARCUS TULLIS

Step Photography
ERIN BASSETT

Production
J. ARTHUR MEDIA

Vice President
TRISHA MALCOLM

Publisher
CAROLINE KILMER

Creative Director
DIANE LAMPHRON

Production Manager
DAVID JOINNIDES

President
ART JOINNIDES

Chairman
JAY STEIN

This book is dedicated to the woman who gave me a love of all things creative. Thank you, Grandma Sharon.

Library of Congress Cataloging-in-Publication Data

Names: Bassett, Erin, author.

Title: The Art of Bible Journaling : More Than 60 Step-by-Step Techniques for Expressing Your Faith Creatively / by Erin Bassett.

Description: First edition. | New York : Get Creative 6, 2017. | Includes index.

Identifiers: LCCN 2017003451 | ISBN 9781942021827 (pbk.)

Subjects: LCSH: Spiritual journals—Authorship. | Bible crafts.

Classification: LCC BL628.5 .B37 2017 | DDC 248.4/6—dc23

LC record available at https://lccn.loc.gov/2017003451

Manufactured in China

1 3 5 7 9 10 8 6 4 2

First Edition

About the Author

Erin Bassett lives in Southern California with her husband, two dogs, and a new kitten. She is blessed to be the aunt of five children and spends as much time as possible with them, often working on art projects. Erin is an art and crafts addict who has been working as a craft designer and artist for many years. She enjoys sharing her love of all things artsy on her creativitE blog (erinbassett.com) and in the classes she teaches. Erin has had many of her projects published in various magazines and books, works with several manufacturers, and considers it a blessing to be able to call her passion "work." She is the substitute teaching leader of her local Bible Study Fellowship (bsfinternational.org) class and leads a women's Sunday school class.

Acknowledgments

"Everybody born comes from the Creator trailing wisps of glory. We come from the Creator with creativity." —Maya Angelou.

To the Ultimate Creator and my Savior: Thank you for sacrificing Yourself for Your creation. Your humility and example inspire me to serve You with my life by loving people and sharing You with them. May You receive all the honor and glory for all that You have done in my life.

To my family: Shew, it's over! Thank you for putting up with all of the loooong hours, Crock-Pot meals, and lack of clean clothes while I worked on this book. I love you!

To my dogs: I definitely will be making up for all the walks we've missed!

To my friends: You give me so much encouragement! Marian, Ann, Dana, Steph, Sharon, Becky, and Lori, thank you for holding me up all the times I doubted myself and for being some of my biggest cheerleaders. I'm honored to call you friends.

To the team: It truly takes a team to create a book, and I'm so thankful that God brought each of you into my life for this project. Joan, Michelle, Irene, and everyone else who had a part in this book, I know you have worked countless hours editing, photographing, designing, and doing all the little things that need to get done to pull this together. Thank you for pouring your life into this so other people can get to know Jesus better.

Contents

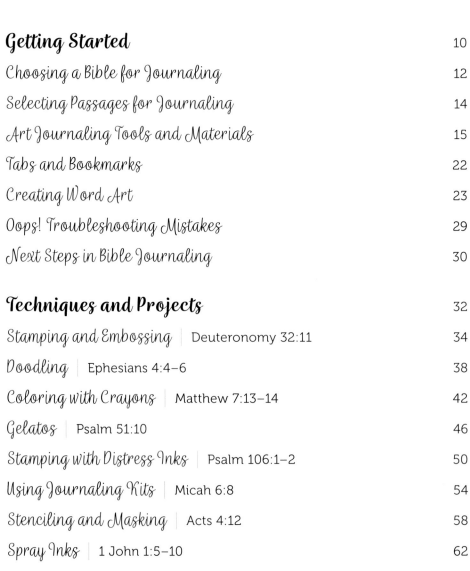

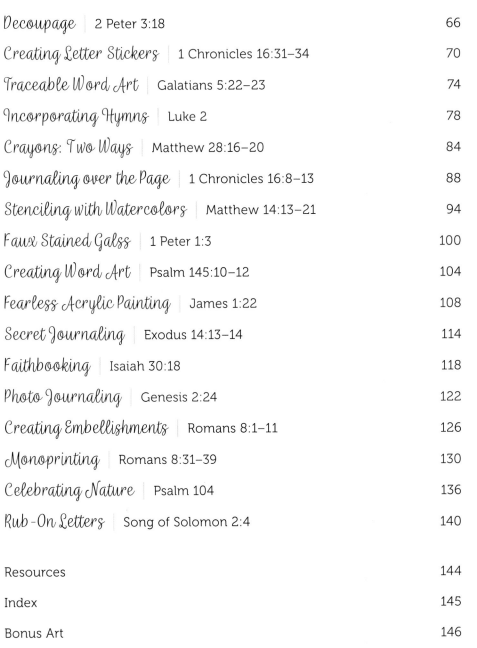

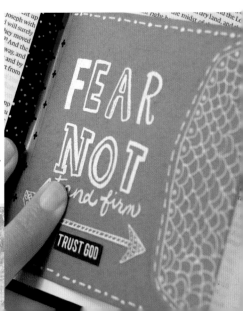

Introduction

Thanks to a grandma who loved to involve me in her sewing, crafts, and cooking activities, I was introduced early on to a multitude of ways to be creative. What had always been fun as a kid, and at times a lifeline to my sanity, evolved into one of the ways I worship the Lord as an adult. Looking back now it seems like a natural progression to go from creating artwork just for me before I decided to follow Jesus to expressing myself artistically before the King of Kings once I knew Him.

As a child I enjoyed the occasional times my family attended church and was drawn to know more about God. But, being a kid and not hearing the Bible or any explanation of it regularly, it was hard for me to fully grasp what the Bible said. After memorizing John 3:16, I remember asking one of the Sunday school teachers how we could have eternal life when I knew family members who had died and were no longer with us. I don't recall what she told me, but I know I didn't understand her explanation.

Fast-forward to my teenage years, the first day of school, in a new town where I knew no one. The first person I met at the school bus stop told me her sister was dragging her to a church youth group that night and asked if I wanted to go. Not knowing another soul my age in town, I jumped at any chance to connect with other teens. So I went to the event, and, long story short, it changed my life. When the youth pastor spoke about what the Bible said about having a relationship with God, for the first time I understood how I was created in the image of God. I learned that even if we are good people, by God's standards we have no chance of getting into Heaven on our own, because sin had entered the world and the hearts of men and women. That God had come down to Earth as a baby and lived a sinless life so that one day He could die on the cross to redeem me and allow me to have an eternal relationship with God.

That night when I got home I couldn't stop thinking about that message. I dug out a Bible we had and searched for the verses that were shared that night. I prayed to Him and confessed that I was a sinner and that I was putting my faith in Jesus as the only way to salvation. I then committed myself to Him, allowing Him to rule my heart.

That decision began my study of God's Word. Over the years I did various Bible studies and attended church services, all the while jotting down notes in the tiny margins of my Bible. I used certain highlighter colors to signify different themes I came across. I made symbols and drawings to help me remember what different concepts meant. I underlined and circled important words and phrases that spoke to me. Technically, I guess that means I've been putting art in my Bible since day one of becoming a Christian.

I've always been involved in art and crafting, so it was natural for my note-taking and highlighting to evolve into more involved art journaling as a way to connect with God's Word. But I know that many other Christians have not had the same experiences of writing and drawing in their Bibles, and the thought of actually doing so may seem taboo. Know this: I love God's Word and I truly believe that it is inspired by God. I believe that to write or not to write in the Bible is a decision that needs to be made between the individual and the Lord. If you believe that you shouldn't mark in your Bible, don't. Apply the techniques in this book to blank art journal pages instead of your Bible. However, if after diligently praying about it, you feel that it is a way to glorify the Lord and meditate in His Word, then by all means follow along.

The purpose of Bible art journaling is not to have fun and show off one's artwork; it's to draw yourself closer to His Word and interact meaningfully with the Bible. Often journalers use it alongside a traditional Bible study or in addition to their personal devotion time. It is *not* a replacement for deeper Bible study; it's an accompaniment to it. It's a way to record what is meaningful and inspiring to you. Over time, you can look back over your Bibles full of art and see reminders of how you've grown along your journey as a believer and see the blessings, answered prayers, and ways in which God has led you through hard times.

Bible art journaling is also a fantastic way to meditate on scripture and commit verses to memory, because you really focus on each individual word as you sketch out verses to create word art, choose letter stickers, or stamp key words. By creating a visual reminder about that portion of scripture, those of us who are visual learners will be more likely to remember the verses and their meaning.

Whatever your reasons for starting or continuing Bible art journaling, I hope you will find my experiences, techniques, and ideas I share in this book to be an inspiration and a starting point for your own artful journey in discovering God's word.

THE LETTER OF PAUL TO THE
ROMANS

Greeting

1 Paul, a servant[1] of Christ Jesus, called to be an apostle, set apart for the gospel of God, [2] which he promised beforehand through his prophets in the holy Scriptures, [3] concerning his Son, who was descended from David[2] according to the flesh [4] and was declared to be the Son of God in power according to the Spirit of holiness by his resurrection from the dead, Jesus Christ our Lord, [5] through whom we have received grace and apostleship to bring about the obedience of faith for the sake of his name among all the nations, [6] including you who are called to belong to Jesus Christ,

[7] To all those in Rome who are loved by God and called to be saints:

Grace to you and peace from God our Father and the Lord Jesus Christ.

Longing to Go to Rome

[8] First, I thank my God through Jesus Christ for all of you, because your faith is proclaimed in all the world. [9] For God is my witness, whom I serve with my spirit in the gospel of his Son, that without ceasing I mention you [10] always in my prayers, asking that somehow by God's will I may now at last succeed in coming to you. [11] For I long to see you, that I may impart to you some spiritual gift to strengthen you— [12] that is, that we may be mutually encouraged by each other's faith, both yours and mine. [13] I do not want you to be unaware, brothers,[3] that I have often intended to come to you (but thus far have been prevented), in order that I may reap some harvest among you as well as among the rest of the Gentiles. [14] I am under obligation both to Greeks and to barbarians,[4] both to the wise and to the foolish. [15] So I am eager to preach the gospel to you also who are in Rome.

The Righteous Shall Live by Faith

[16] For I am not ashamed of the gospel, for it is the power of God for salvation to everyone who believes, to the Jew first and also to the Greek. [17] For in it the righteousness of God is revealed from faith for faith,[5] as it is written, "The righteous shall live by faith."[6]

God's Wrath on Unrighteousness

[18] For the wrath of God is revealed from heaven against all ungodliness and unrighteousness of men, who by their unrighteousness suppress the truth. [19] For what can be known about God is plain to them, because God has shown it to them. [20] For his invisible attributes, namely, his eternal power and divine nature, have been clearly perceived, ever since the creation of the world,[7] in the things that have been made. So they are without excuse. [21] For although they knew God, they did not honor him as God or give thanks to him, but they became futile in their thinking, and their foolish hearts were darkened. [22] Claiming to be wise, they became fools, [23] and exchanged the glory of the immortal God for images resembling mortal man and birds and animals and creeping things.

[24] Therefore God gave them up in the lusts of their hearts to impurity, to the dishonoring of their bodies among themselves, [25] because they exchanged the truth about

[for a lie and worshiped and served the creature rather than the [Creator], who is] blessed forever! Amen.

[26] For this reason God gave them up to dishonorable passions. [For] exchanged natural relations for those that are contrary to nature; [27] [and the men like] wise gave up natural relations with women and were consumed wi[th passion for one] another, men committing shameless acts with men and receiving [in themselves the] due penalty for their error.

[28] And since they did not see fit to acknowledge God, God [gave them up to a] debased mind to do what ought not to be done. [29] They were fill[ed with all manner] of unrighteousness, evil, covetousness, malice. They are full of [envy, murder, strife,] deceit, maliciousness. They are gossips, [30] slanderers, haters of Go[d, insolent, haughty,] boastful, inventors of evil, disobedient to parents, [31] foolish, faith[less, heartless, ruth]less. [32] Though they know God's righteous decree that those who [practice such things] deserve to die, they not only do them but give approval to those [who practice them.]

God's Righteous Judgment

2 Therefore you have no excuse, O man, every one of you w[ho passes judgment. For] ing judgment on another you condemn yourself, because [you, the judge,] practice such things. [3] Do you suppose, O man—you who judg[e those who] things and yet do them yourself—that you will escape the j[udgment of God?] [4] Or do you presume on the riches of his kindness and forbearance a[nd patience, not knowing] that God's kindness is meant to lead you to repentance? [5] Bu[t because of your hard and] impenitent heart you are storing up wrath for yourself on the [day of wrath when God's] righteous judgment will be revealed.

[6] He will render to each one according to his works: [7] t[o those who by patience in] well-doing seek for glory and honor and immortality, he w[ill give eternal life;] [8] but for those who are self-seeking[1] and do not obey the truth, but [obey unrighteousness, there] will be wrath and fury. [9] There will be tribulation and dis[tress for every human being] who does evil, the Jew first and also the Greek, [10] but gl[ory and honor and peace for] everyone who does good, the Jew first and also the Greek.

God's Judgment and the Law

[12] For all who have sinned without the law will also [perish without the law, and all] who have sinned under the law will be judged by the la[w. 13 For it is not the hearers of] the law who are righteous before God, but the doers [of the law who will be justified.] [14] For when Gentiles, who do not have the law, by natu[re do what the law requires, they] are a law to themselves, even though they do not hav[e the law. 15 They show that the] work of the law is written on their hearts, while their [conscience also bears witness, and] their conflicting thoughts accuse or even excuse the[m 16 on that day when, according] to my gospel, God judges the secrets of men by Chr[ist Jesus.]

[17] But if you call yourself a Jew and rely on the law [and boast in God 18 and know his] will and approve what is excellent, because you are i[nstructed from the law; 19 and if you] are sure that you yourself are a guide to the blind, a [light to those who are in darkness,] [20] an instructor of the foolish, a teacher of children [having in the law the embodiment] of knowledge and truth— [21] you then who teach [others, do you not teach yourself?] While you preach against stealing, do you steal[? 22 You who say that one must not] commit adultery, do you commit adultery? You w[ho abhor idols, do you rob temples?] [23] You who boast in the law dishonor God by bre[aking the law. 24 For, as it is written,] "The name of God is blasphemed among the Ge[ntiles because of you."]

[25] For circumcision indeed is of value if you [obey the law, but if you break the law,] your circumcision becomes uncircumcision. [26] S[o, if a man who is uncircumcised keeps] the precepts of the law, will not his uncircu[mcision be regarded as circumcision?]

[1] Or slave (for the contextual rendering of the Greek word doulos, see Preface) [2] Or who came from the offspring of David [3] Or brothers and sisters. The plural Greek word adelphoi (translated "brothers") refers to siblings in a family. In New Testament usage, depending on the context, adelphoi may refer either to men or to both men and women who are siblings (brothers and sisters) in God's family, the church. [4] That is, non-Greeks [5] Or beginning and ending in faith [6] Or The one who by faith is righteous shall live [7] Or clearly perceived from the creation of the world [a] Hab. 2:4

[1] Or contentious [2] Or counted [a] Isa. 52:5

Getting Started

If you're new to Bible art journaling, you might have questions about where to begin. Which Bible should you use? Do you need to raid the local art-supply store just to get started? Which passages should you journal about? If you have already begun your Bible journaling journey, you might have encountered problems and questions or you might be looking for new ways to express your faith creatively. In this section, I'll try to answer these questions and prepare you to jump into the Bible journaling techniques and projects described in the second part of the book. What are you waiting for? Let's get started!

Choosing a Bible for Journaling

Selecting a Bible to work in may seem like a daunting task because there are so many translations, and each one is published in multiple forms.

The good news is that there have never been so many options for Bibles to use for art journaling. Here is an overview of what's available.

Translations

Your local church or denomination may have a preference for which translation you use. Likewise, if you study the Bible already you probably have a favorite Bible translation you feel most comfortable with. For me, it's the English Standard Version (ESV) Bible, but I do refer to other versions at times because seeing a different translation sometimes gives me a fuller idea of the author's intent.

If you have never given much thought to which translation to use, now may be the time to take a look at the wide range of choices available to you. The Old Testament section of the Bible was originally written in Hebrew and Aramaic, and the New Testament was written in Greek, so the Bible needed to be translated into English.

Translation Methods

There are four distinct methods with which the majority of versions are translated.

- **Verbal equivalence:** This is translated with a strong preference for using the same word order as the original text.

- **Dynamic equivalence:** This is translated with freedom to rearrange the word order to improve readability.

- **Hybrid:** This is a combined approach in which Bible scholars decide which method to use in each situation they come across.

- **Paraphrase:** This is translated thought for thought and allows

freedom to rearrange or use different, more modern words to convey the meaning of the verses.

Tips for Choosing a Translation

When searching for which version to use, ask the Lord to help guide you as you seek His truth.

- **Seek the advice of wise people like your pastor.** Just because a version is popular doesn't necessarily mean it's the most accurate.

- **Go to one of the many websites or applications that will allow you to compare versions of the Bible.** Look at the same verse in both translations you are considering and see which one is the best fit for you.

- **Consider which type of translation you're looking for as an art journal.** This may be different than your everyday study Bible.

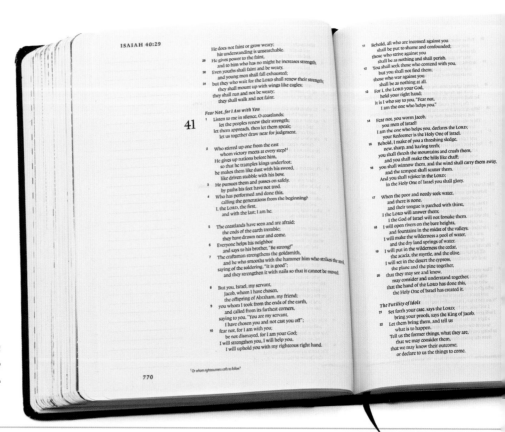

Journaling Bibles (left) leave a wide margin on each page, while interleaved Bibles (right) alternate scripture with full blank pages.

- **Before making your purchase, read the preface of the Bible.** It will explain how it was translated and whether it is a literal or thought-for-thought translation.

Types of Journaling Bibles

According to the Evangelical Christian Publishers Association, the top five best-selling Bible translations for 2016 were the New International Version (NIV), the New Living Translation (NLV), the King James Version (KJV), the New King James Version (NKJV), and the English Standard Version (ESV). These are the versions that are most likely to have editions designed to accommodate Bible journaling.

Journaling and Note-Taking Bibles

The major pro of using a Bible of this style in your chosen translation is that they usually have wider margins than traditional Bibles. The one I use has a 2-inch (5 cm) lined side margin. The lines are just faint enough that I barely notice them; however, they are really helpful for lining things up or for having consistent height when hand lettering. You can choose a Bible with either a single column of text per page or two columns per page like most traditional styles of Bibles. I prefer single column because it allows me to clearly focus on the passage that the Lord is nudging me to focus my art on.

Interleaved Bibles

This style of Bible is fairly new to me and I recently purchased one to use for art journaling. Blank pages are inserted in between each page of scripture so you have plenty of room to work and don't have to be concerned with obscuring God's words.

Creative Bibles

A creative Bible is a merger of a Bible and a coloring book. Because they already have line art in them, they are a good way for a timid journaler to ease into Bible art journaling. However, because the designs are already made, they are what the illustrator was inspired to create, not what God is speaking to you about in His Word, so they are not my preferred version.

Can You Use a Standard Bible?

Definitely! In fact, that's how many of us got started with combining words and illustrations in our Bibles. Your margin space is limited, but think of it as a creative challenge and ask the Lord to help you glorify Him in what you create.

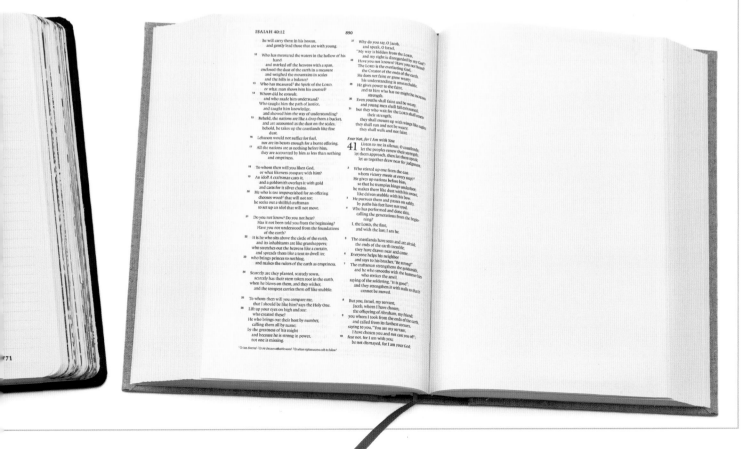

Selecting Passages for Journaling

I'm sure everyone's process of Bible art journaling and the amount of time they devote to it are different, but here is how I approach choosing a verse or verses to journal about. I study a portion of scripture in my regular study of the Bible, so I know the full meaning and context of that portion of the Bible. I then choose the portion of (or sometimes all of) the verses that God spoke to me about and create a page about it. If I don't have time to create a page, I just put a sticky note in my Bible study notebook so I know to look there when I do have extra time.

Next, I pray. I ask the Holy Spirit to help me remember His Word and motivate me to be obedient to what I've read. Then I grab a mug of tea or coffee, turn on some Christian music, and think about how I could best illustrate these verses to help me remember them. I then get to work.

Here are some other ideas for choosing passages in your Bible to art journal:

- Use a concordance (an alphabetical listing of words and phrases that shows where the terms occur in the scripture) to look up all the verses that contain a certain word and see what the Lord leads you to journal about.

- Is a Christian holiday coming up? Do an advent study about the birth of Christ, study about the timeline of Jesus's death and resurrection, or do a page on gratitude for Thanksgiving.

- Join a Bible study group and journal the verses you're studying.

- Journal sermons from church services.

Which Themes Speak to You?

If I look back at the study Bibles I've used over the years, I can easily see that certain Biblical themes really mean a lot to me. I've underlined, highlighted, and made notes about them as I studied God's Word. Themes such as God's everlasting love, the human (my) heart, and waiting on the Lord's timing all mean a lot to me as I mature as a follower of Christ. I'm sure if you've studied the Bible for some time you have themes that keep drawing you in as well. Looking for those themes is a great way to spark ideas for journaling pages.

Art Journaling Tools and Materials

Let's talk supplies. If you're new to Bible journaling, what do you really need to get started? Ultimately, I think you could get by with just the Lord, your Bible, and a pen. The best way to gauge what you need beyond that is to think about what you actually plan on doing in your Bible. Do you like to doodle? Are you a painter? A scrapbooker? Or is computer-generated art your thing?

Start by taking inventory of what you already have that you can use. You probably own scissors, rulers, pencils, or pens. Children's art supplies are great to use; just make sure they're acid free if you're concerned about the longevity of your Bible. If you can't afford to buy new supplies, challenge yourself to think of new ways to use the ones you have.

Below, I've listed and described the tools and materials I use most often in my Bible art journal and which I demonstrate in the projects in this book. My lists are by no means exhaustive; there are hundreds of other supplies that are fun to use. These are suggested products to look into using if you desire and are able. These recommendations are not the only, or the best ones, for *you*. We all have personal preferences, and I won't be offended if you like a different brand or product than I use!

Must-Haves

These are the materials that just about everyone will need and use fairly regularly when Bible journaling.

Ruler

I like to eyeball measurements and I'm okay with having hand-drawn lines that are not perfectly straight, but I still use a ruler for certain tasks. For measuring and for drawing those sometimes necessary, perfectly straight lines, I use a traditional steel ruler, as it won't bend, warp, or get nicked.

For centering or for laying down letter stickers, I like to use the see-through Pro Centering Acrylic Craft Ruler made by EK Success. The markings on the ruler make it really quick and easy to adhere papers and stickers as well as to make sure your hand lettering is centered and straight.

Pencils and Erasers

Whether you're sketching out drawings and word art or just marking a measurement on your page, you're going to need a pencil and a good eraser. You can certainly use standard pencils with erasers, but I find that they leave too thick and dark of a mark and they're hard to completely erase. I prefer a mechanical pencil because it stays sharp. Perfection Eraser Pencil from Faber-Castell erases everything from pencil to some inks. For large areas of erasing I like to use the Faber-Castell Dust-Free Eraser.

Markers and Pens for Lettering and Drawing

There are thousands of choices of pens and markers, and it can be downright overwhelming for a newbie to try to figure out what to buy. It really is important to choose ones that won't bleed through the ultra-thin pages of a Bible.

Many types of pens are available in different-size nibs, or tips, and each nib will change the feel of how it writes and the amount of ink that flows. Having nib options is great if you're adding hand lettering to your pages or want to vary the size of lines on your drawings and doodles.

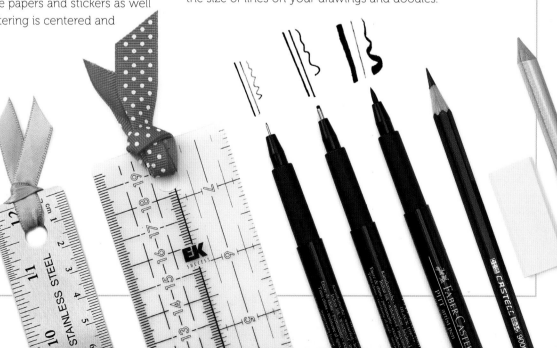

The pens I use most for doodling, line drawings, and lettering are Faber-Castell PITT Artist Pens. They contain India ink, which is permanent, water resistant, and resists fading when dry. They come in a variety of sizes and nibs, including brush and calligraphy.

Staedtler Triplus Fineliner Pens only come with a fine .3mm nib, but if you happen to leave them uncapped for a couple of days, they won't dry out. I also love that they are less likely to bleed though my pages and they write well over paint.

Two brush pens I like to use for hand lettering are Sakura Pigma Professional and Tombow Fudenosuke. Their brushes have the perfect amount of give that makes writing with them easier than pens that have a super-soft brush.

I've tried a countless number of white pens, and my favorite is the Uni-ball Signo white gel pen, because the ink comes out so smoothly. I use them so much that I always get the big pack of them! The white Faber-Castell Big Brush Marker has a large brush tip and is waterproof when dry.

Scissors

You probably already have some at your disposal to use. As long as they are sharp and have a pointed tip, they should work fine for many of the items you may be likely to add to your Bible.

Crayons

These are not a necessity, but because you may have some in your home already, don't discount using them on your Bible pages. You might think crayons will make your pages look childish, but they won't and are a great, inexpensive way to add color.

Colored Pencils

Colored pencils provide beautiful color and are easy to travel with, even if it's just to the living room couch. Quality and price vary on these, and they are one of

those you-get-what-you-pay-for items. The less-expensive ones we used as kids aren't very vibrant, but they're usable if that's all you have or can afford. I've found the more expensive ones to be more vibrant and to blend better. My favorite colored pencils are Prismacolor Premier; their Mixed Media Set is a great collection to start with.

Light Box

A small, inexpensive light box makes it easy to trace fonts, sketches, and other items directly into your Bible. There are ways to get around using a light box, such as substituting a tablet device or holding your paper to a window.

Adhesives

If you plan to add papers or other items to your pages, you will need adhesive. When buying adhesives, look for acid-free varieties. There is a different type of adhesive for just about every use under the sun, but these are the ones I use most often:

- **Dry adhesive:** Scotch Advanced Tape Glider (ATG) Adhesive Tape. I use this in my Advanced Tape Glider, which is sold separately.

- **Wet adhesive:** Tombow Mono Multi Liquid Glue.

- **Glue sticks:** The Elmer's ones you used in school work great and are acid free; Ranger and Xyron have glue sticks created for the scrapbooking and mixed-media industries.

Beyond Basics

If you want to create a little more pizzazz on your pages, here are some items you may want to add to your stash.

Craft Mat and/or Palette Paper

Craft mats are a fantastic way to protect your work surface. Because they are nonstick and nonporous, messes can be easily wiped off when wet and scraped off when dry. They withstand high heat as well, so they are great to have under your work while you're using a heat gun. Craft mats can be used as palette for your paints, but if you'd like a disposable option, a pad of palette paper is very convenient.

Gesso

Gesso is a primer for paper, canvas, and other substrates. For Bible journaling, I sometimes use clear gesso to seal the pages and prevent paint and other materials from leaking through. Gesso comes in different consistencies and textures. I prefer to use a thinner, smooth gesso because it won't add much bulk to the paper and will be easy to work

Applying a thin layer of clear gesso to your page will help prevent paint and other wet mediums from bleeding through.

with. My favorite brands of clear gesso are Prima Marketing's Art Basics and Ranger's Dina Wakley Media Clear Gesso.

Colored Markers and Pens

You may want to steer clear of using these directly on your untreated pages until you're familiar with using them on thin Bible pages, especially if having them bleed through the page will make you sad. It's been my experience that you need to protect your page with clear gesso primer if you really want to avoid bleed-through.

Pigma Micron, Faber-Castell PITT Artist Pens or Big Brush Markers, and Illustrated Faith Markers are great permanent, waterproof, and archival ink marker choices. If using them directly on an untreated page, use light pressure and avoiding coloring over the same spot, which could lead to bleed-through.

Although water-based markers aren't waterproof, they are a really fun way to add color to pages. My preferred water-based markers are Tombow Dual Brush Pens and Kuretake Zig Art & Graphic Twin Markers.

Gel Pens

I have a love/hate relationship with gel pens. When they are brand new, they are wonderful, colorful pens to use on your artwork. They glide easily over paper and most acrylic paints, and some even have an embossed look to them when dry. However, once you stop using them for a while they tend to dry out and become unusable. I've had the fewest issues with Sakura Gelly Roll gel pens. Avoid buying the least-expensive generic ones because they tend to have a short life span.

Stamps

There are many stamps on the market today—many of them faith-based and many more with general themes. They can be made out of rubber, clear acrylic, or foam and are a great way to add designs to your pages. Some of my favorite faith-based stamps are made by Dare 2B Artzy. For traditional stamps, I like those made by Hero Arts, Ranger, and Altenew.

I use alphabet stamps often, and many people like to date their pages with a date stamp, too.

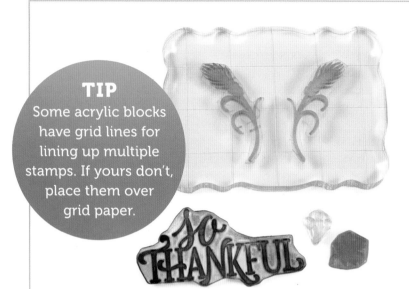

Acrylic Blocks or MISTI

If you use acrylic stamps, you will need to mount them on an acrylic block or other plastic item, such as an old CD case or the lid to your stamp ink.

Acrylic blocks often come in sets, but they can be purchased individually as well if you want to add to your collection as needed. Make sure you get ones that will accommodate your stamp size needs.

MISTI, the Most Incredible Stamp Tool Invented, from My Sweet Petunia, is a precision stamp tool. It really cuts down on the unpredictability of stamping. (See page 51 for instructions on using the MISTI.) The MISTI comes in several sizes. The mini works well for stamping Bible pages. Other manufacturers now produce similar tools.

Stamp Ink

If you plan to use a wet medium on top of or next to the stamped image, choose a permanent ink so it doesn't run and always make sure the ink is completely dry before using

other products on the page. Also, like markers, some inks have a tendency to bleed through the page. Prep your page with clear gesso if you're worried about bleed-through. My preferred brands of permanent ink are Tsukineko's StazOn Solvent Ink and their Memento Ink. My favorite brands of water-based ink are ClearSnap, Stampin' Up!, and Distress Ink.

Chalk ink is a matte ink that dries quickly and is archival. Many brands are permanent when heat set. I most often use ClearSnap, specifically their Petal Point and Cat's Eye ink pads, and Quick Quotes Powder Puff Chalking Ink pads.

Wet-Embossing Powder and Ink

Wet embossing is a technique is which you use a heat gun to heat up and melt embossing powder that is adhered to your paper with embossing ink. My favorite clear embossing

To emboss a stamped design, follow these basic steps: 1) place the acrylic stamp on the acrylic block, 2) ink the stamp with embossing ink, 3) stamp the design on your page, 4) pour embossing powder on the design while wet, 5) pour off the excess powder, and 6) melt the powder with a heat gun.

ink is Tsukineko's VersaMark Watermark Stamp Pad. You can use any color pigment ink pad if you plan on using a clear embossing powder.

The clear embossing powder I like to use is Stampin' Emboss Powder from Stampin' Up! for fine, detailed projects and Melt Art's Ultra Thick Embossing Enamel for a heavier embossed effect.

WOW! Embossing Powers are double treated for static, so you have fewer random bits of powder sticking to areas you don't want to emboss. For other brands of embossing powder, you can use an Embossing Buddy from Stampin' Up!, a little sachet filled with a powder that reduces static and prevents stray powder from sticking to areas without ink. Just rub it over the paper before stamping onto it.

Craft Heat Gun

If you're going to wet emboss or are just impatient and want to dry paint and other mediums more quickly, you will want to invest in a craft heat gun. The Ranger Heat It Craft Tool is quiet and effective. My favorite is from Marvy Uchida, even though it's louder.

Spray Ink

If you want a pop of unstructured color on your page, spray ink is just the thing to use, although it can be a bit tricky to control. You can spray it directly onto a page or use it in combination with stencils or masks. See page 63 for more tips on working with spray inks.

Watercolor Paints

While you can invest in artist-quality watercolors, the ones you used as a child will work just fine in your Bible. I've used both Crayola and Artist's Loft brands successfully. If you're planning on upgrading your paint set, try Sakura's Koi Field Set. This 24-color set is a fantastic size to use at home or when traveling. I've even used it while flying!

Brushes

As an artist, I have a considerable collection of paintbrushes, but the one I use most of the time for Bible journaling is a water brush. Water brushes come in different brush sizes and contain a water reservoir attached to the brush. My favorite water brushes are the Kuretake Fude Water Brush Pens and the Pentel Arts Aquash Water Brushes.

Foam brushes are inexpensive and perfect for applying gesso or stenciling.

Paper Trimmer

Scissors may come in handy, but if you plan on adding any papers to your Bible you may want to invest in a paper trimmer, which makes straight cuts incredibly easy. Some good brands to test out first are Fiskars and Westcott.

Stickers and Rub-Ons

If you're uncomfortable with using your own handwriting on your Bible pages or if you just like to vary the way your pages look, letter stickers or rub-ons are great options. These days there are so many diverse styles of alphabet, word, and phrase stickers and rub-ons available in craft stores that it's easy to get carried away with buying them. There are also plenty of beautifully created stickers and rub-ons of design elements and motifs. (This book includes two sheets of bonus stickers at the back.)

Patterned Papers

Thanks to the scrapbooking industry, craft stores abound with a countless number of patterned papers. Many are themed or are coordinated to be used with other papers in the same collection. Patterned papers come in a variety of sizes. For Bible journaling, 6" x 6" (15 x 15 cm) pads are a economical way to get a variety of coordinating papers with smaller-scale patterns.

Just for Fun

Are you ready to move on to the tools and mediums that definitely aren't necessities but are certainly fun to use? Here are some great ones to get you started.

Watercolor Pencils or Water-Soluble Crayons

These are a hybrid of two amazing mediums: watercolors and colored pencils or crayons. You start by coloring all of, or a section of, your design and then use a wet brush to move and blend the color out. When finished, it looks like you used watercolor paint. These are fun to play with if you want to experiment beyond watercolors. My favorite brand of watercolor pencils is Faber-Castell's Art GRIP Aquarelle, and my go-to watercolor crayons are Caran d'Ache Classic Neocolor II and Reeves Water Soluble Wax Pastels.

Upgraded Crayons

Give your regular old crayons to the kids in your life and move on to highly pigmented wax crayons that have a smooth barrel that the crayons twist out of and that can be sharpened with a regular pencil sharpener. Faber-Castell's Paper Crafter Crayons are my favorite ones, but if you're looking for a less expensive option, Crayola also makes twistable crayons.

Gelatos

These are by far one of my most-used mediums for putting color on Bible pages and in mixed-media art projects. What may look like colored lip balm at a glance is really a pigment stick that can be easily blended with or without water and is so creamy and smooth. Faber-Castell manufactures them. See page 46 for ideas on working with Gelatos.

Acrylic Paint

Acrylic paint comes in a variety of viscosities, or thicknesses, and all of them can be used in your Bible. Craft paints are fine to use in your Bible. They are budget friendly and come in many shades. My favorite brand of craft paints is DecoArt Americana acrylics. Professional-quality acrylic paints are more expensive, but contain more fine pigment and are typically more vivid, even when watered down.

Water can be added to any acrylic paint so that it will be more translucent, which will give you a completely different look than using it straight out of the tube. Just be mindful that the higher the water content, the more likely it is to wrinkle your pages. The professional-quality acrylic paints I use most often are made by Golden and Liquitex.

Waxed Deli Paper

This type of paper is very thin, although it's thicker than tissue paper. When you adhere deli paper with artwork on it to your page, the deli paper itself virtually melts into the page, leaving artwork showing. I purchase deli paper from a restaurant  supply store. Deli paper can be painted, written, stamped, and even printed on. I like to use it with a Gelli Arts Gel Printing Plate.

Gelli Arts Gel Printing Plate

Gelli printing is a fun way to print on your Bible pages. Gelli Plates come in a variety of shapes and sizes and they look and feel like gelatin, although they don't contain gelatin or

Mark-Making Tools

These are items you probably have around the house that you can use to make marks in paint. Toilet paper tubes, sponges, old hotel room key cards, punchinella (the waste left behind when sequins are punched out), and bubble wrap are just a few items that create interesting textures.

Ephemera

If you're a memory keeper, chances are you already saved that church bulletin or tag off your tea bag with the great quote on it, but if you never thought of adding those bits and pieces of everyday life to your Bible, keep your eyes open for pretty, fun, or meaningful ephemera you can use.

Embellishments

Washi tape, sequins, ribbons, dried flowers, and other dimensional pieces can add a great look to your page. Just keep in mind that your Bible wasn't made to be chock full of these pieces, so the spine can't accommodate a lot of bulk on every page. Also, having too bulky of an item on a page will make it hard to create future pages on top of it.

Washi tape is a versatile embellishment that comes in a huge variety of colors and patterns.

Specialty Computer Printer Papers

I am the first to admit I'm a digi-girl. I love technology, computers, and all the geeky stuff, so using my computer for Bible art journaling comes naturally for me.

Two of my favorite "papers" to print on are clear sticker paper and transparencies. Because you can create or purchase so many fabulous designs, it's really handy to be able to quickly print out something to use in your Bible, especially if it's 2 a.m. and all the craft stores are closed.

Die-Cutting Machine

Both manual and high-tech digital die-cutting machines are great tools to have in your arsenal. Use them to create your own stencils and masks, cut out embellishments, or cut around your favorite stamped images to add to your Bible.

any other animal products. To use the Gelli Plate, apply acrylic paint or printmaking ink to it and then make designs or marks in it while adding other colors of paint. When finished, press a paper onto it, transferring the print.

Stencils and Masks

There are so many ways to use stencils and masks. No matter your design aesthetic, you are sure to find a plethora of stencils and masks that are just right for you. They can be used with just about every art medium, so you can get a lot of different looks, even with the same stencil or mask. You can apply paint or ink over them, trace around them with markers or colored pencils, or use them like a stamp by applying the medium to them and pressing them onto paper. A couple of my favorite stencil manufacturers are Crafter's Workshop and Stencil Girl.

Tabs and Bookmarks

Many Bible art journalers like to mark a page they have journaled with a tab or bookmark. These are a handy way to locate pages you want to revisit, and they can add another visual element to the page. Premade tabs and bookmarks can be found at your local Bible bookstore or online at Amazon or Etsy. If you have a die-cutting machine, you may want to invest in a tab die (or cut-file). We've included some die-cut tabs at the back of this book that you can use on your pages, as well as stencils on the back flap that can be traced on card stock and cut

out. If you're new to studying God's Word, it may be helpful to mark the books of the Bible with tabs. We've provided sticker tabs with the names of the books of the Bible.

Bookmarks are just an extra cherry-on-top sort of item to add to your pages because they not only mark your spot but are pretty darn cute. There are tons of manufactured ones available at scrapbooking, art-supply, craft, or office-supply stores. Making bookmarks is really fun, too, and can be as simple as adding a ribbon bow to a paper clip or sandwiching the page with two identical stickers.

From left to right: For this bookmark, I added a word sticker to a paper tab and stapled it together with a ribbon. To create the Christmas tab, I added a sticker to a tab and attached it to the page with washi tape for another bit of color and pattern. At the back of this book, you'll find sticker tabs with the names of the books of the Bible.

Creating Word Art

I am a sketcher and a doodler. I do it when I'm on the phone, while taking notes in a meeting, and in my mixed-media art journals. You may be thinking, "Great, I am *so not* a sketcher, so I'll skip this part!" Bear with me a minute. Are you labeling yourself this way because you hate drawing and are more of a word person, are afraid to try sketching, or are frustrated because you just can't get it perfect? If doodling and drawing are really not your thing, that's fine; God created us all to be creative, but not all to be creative in the same way. However, if fear of not achieving perfection is holding you back from even trying, and you really do have a desire to grow in that area, go to God in prayer about it. Share your dissatisfaction with Him and ask Him for the patience to stick it out for a set period of time and then reevaluate what to do then. If you're ready to give it a go, here are some ways to get started.

Steps to Creating Word Art

These are the basic steps I follow to create art with words. Practice getting this down first and then graduate to adding in banners or doodles or changing the shape of words.

1. Select a verse or quote you want to use and write it out on a piece of scratch paper or in a notebook.

2. Circle any key words that jump out at you.

3. Give yourself a good amount of space near where you wrote out the verse or quote and measure out your margin dimensions.

4. Decide what style and size you want your key words to be and write those in pencil where you think they will be placed in your practice margin. They can be moved later if they are placed in a problematic spot.

5. Decide what style and size of letters and words you want the supporting words to be and fill those in.

6. Evaluate if it's readable and if it captures what you are trying to communicate. Make changes if necessary. When you're happy with the design, trace it into your Bible.

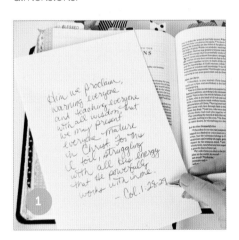

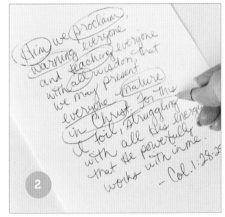

Alphabet Sampler

Hand lettering is an art form in itself, and there are many wonderful books on the market that teach lettering in great detail. Here are a few alphabets you can use to practice lettering and ideas for adding variety to your lettering. Feel free to copy or trace the alphabets to kick-start your own hand lettering.

Basic Alphabet
Start with something like this simple printed alphabet to get your lettering juices flowing. I like to use basic lettering in combination with script and other fancier lettering to balance it.

Aa Bb Cc Dd Ee Ff Gg Hh Ii
Jj Kk Ll Mm Nn Oo Pp Qq Rr
Ss Tt Uu Vv Ww Xx Yy Zz

Script Alphabet
Remember how big a deal it was to learn to write cursive? I'm dismayed to hear that many schools have stopped teaching it. Carefully formed script letters will add a beautiful touch to any Bible page. If your lettering is feeling too ornate, mix it up with some printed lettering.

A B C D E F G H I J K
L M N O P Q R S T U V
W X Y Z a b c d e f g h
i j k l m n o p q r s t
u v w x y z

Mixing Uppercase and Lowercase Letters

Adding variety and interest to your lettering can be as simple as combining uppercase and lowercase letters. Try alternating them or mixing them up more randomly. Here I made them all the same size, but you could also make the lowercase letters smaller.

Variations

Here are some ways I like to play with lettering to personalize it.

- Add curly loops.
- Vary the angles of the letters.
- Mix up the height and/or width of the letters.
- Play with spacing between letters.
- Fill in thicker areas with pattern.
- Add doodles.
- Combine printing and script.

And Another Thing . . .

Have fun with the word *and* in your lettering. Add a fancy ampersand or play with different ways to write out the word. It will become a cute design detail.

Finding Inspiration

Aren't you glad we live in a time when we have so many resources at our disposal? My two favorite ways to find inspiring styles of lettering, words, and the layout of words are online and real-life examples. There are thousands of websites that catalog a huge amount of typography. Look through them. Start creating a file (digital or paper) of those you love. Check out fonts as well and add in those that you would consider using or that inspire you to create a similar look. When you're out and about, take a cell-phone photo of interesting lettering on billboards and signage. If you still receive print publications, rip out examples of cool fonts or word arrangements.

Adding Doodles to Your Word Art

Doodles, or bits of fun artwork, can add so much to the word art in your Bibles. And there are many ways to incorporate them. You can make a prominent banner to place words inside, or you can simply dot your letter *i* with a heart. Here I share some ideas and steps for creating a few of my favorite types of doodles: banners, flowers, and text separators.

Drawing a Banner

Begin with a plan. Do you want your banner to be flat or wavy? Do you want one or both ends to flip around, or dovetail, or will they be anchored to another object? If including words or designs on it, decide the height and width of the banner.

Sketch it in pencil first and then go over the lines with a pen. Allow the ink to fully dry before erasing any remaining pencil lines. If you plan on filling in the design with a water-based medium, be sure to use a waterproof pen.

You can draw a simple, two-dimensional banner like the one shown at left, or follow the steps above to create a banner with ends that flip around. To make it curved, follow the same steps, but curve the horizontal lines.

Drawing Flowers

Although flowers can be used with scripture that refers to God's creation, they are also a pretty way to add visual interest to other passages. Practice drawing different varieties of flowers. They can be drawn realistically or as a doodle. The secret to drawing flowers is to take them step by step. Start with the top layer of petals, then fill in the petals behind them. Add leaves and doodles within the petals to customize them. Look at real flowers in your garden or in photos to get ideas for more shapes and colors.

Basic Flower

Embellished Flower with Leaves

Text Separators

A super-easy way to dress up your word art is to add text separators: decorative lines, squiggles, arrows, and other doodles that help divide up blocks of text or create borders.

You can leave them as line art or color them in with pens or colored pencils. Here are some of my favorites. You're welcome to copy or trace them to use in your word art.

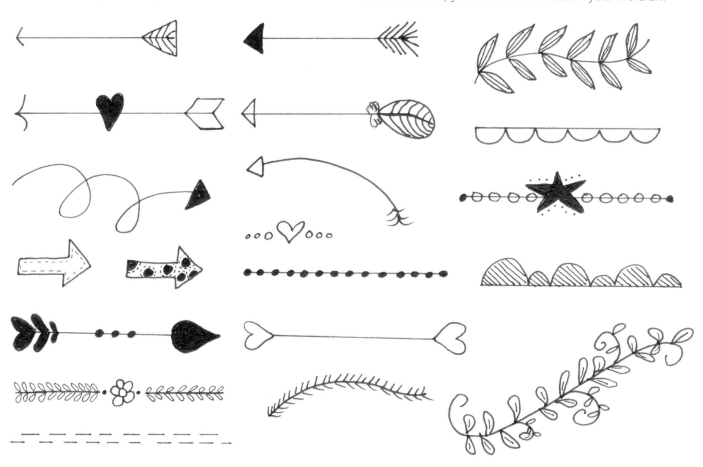

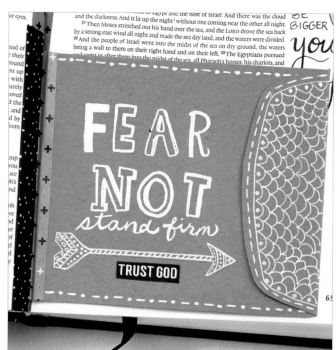

Oops! Troubleshooting Mistakes

One of the things that I hear often from people who want to try Bible art journaling but are afraid to get started is that they're worried they will mess up. I totally understand being anxious about that. I'm sure if Jesus were art journaling, His pages would be perfect. He wouldn't misspell something or be too heavy-handed with paint. You are not Jesus. You will make a mistake and He will still love you anyway. So take a deep breath, ask the Lord to calm your nerves, and get started. When you do make mistakes, which you will, here are some fixes.

Problem: I made a mistake on the Bible page.

Solution: Use a cream (or whatever color your Bible pages are) acrylic paint to fix it (see photos below). For this Bible—the Crossway ESV Single Column Journaling Bible—I use DecoArt Americana paint in light buttermilk. Use a small paintbrush and very little paint. It's better to do two or three light coats than one thick one.

Problem: I made a mistake on top of the background I painted on the Bible page.

Solution: Paint over the mistake using the same color(s) as the background.

Problem: My artwork bled through the page.

Solution: To prevent that from happening, apply a thin coat of clear gesso over the page before you add artwork. If the deed is done, here are a few options:

- Paint over the back of the page with paint that is the same color as the page.
- Lay down a coat of gesso and then create a painted background over it.
- Cut a piece of patterned paper, card stock, or washi tape to cover up the whole margin or just portions of it.

Problem: The page wrinkled.

Solution: Although this isn't always 100 percent fixable, there are ways to smooth it down a bit. If it was caused by having too much water on the page, allow it to dry and then spritz the back of the page with a small mist of water. Use your hands to gently smooth out the wrinkles while it dries.

Some art journalers place a piece of paper over their page and then iron the page flat. For me, I've found that I just end up creating more wrinkles, but you are welcome to try it.

Remember that over time the weight of your Bible may smooth out any remaining waves or wrinkles.

Problem: I fell out of the habit of Bible art journaling.

Solution: The time you spend allowing God's Word to work in your heart is never a waste of time. The Bible is alive and working in the hearts of those who consume and obey it. So let go of the recording playing in your head of failing, let go of feeling overwhelmed, schedule a date with God to journal again, and jump back in!

Problem: I'm just not creative!

Solution: Our Creator has created us in His image and because He is creative, we are creative as well. Turn off that recording in your head that is telling you that you aren't creative. Ask the Holy Spirit to help you tune out beliefs that are untrue and help you see yourself as the Lord does. Remember, too, that your Bible art is a way to glorify God and does not have to be shared with anyone else.

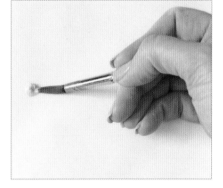
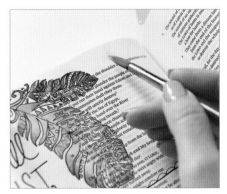

To cover up a stray mark or other mistake, carefully paint over it with a small paintbrush and cream-colored acrylic paint. You'll never know it was there!

Next Steps in Bible Journaling

The Techniques and Projects section of this book includes dozens of ideas for creating art in your Bible. After you've tried creating a few pages, you may be thinking about other ways to artistically express your faith in God's Word.

Covers

To distinguish their journaling Bible from their regular study Bible, many art journalers like to create a cover for it. Many of the techniques and materials demonstrated in the projects in this book can be applied to the cover, including acrylic paint, stickers, and washi tape. If you don't want to alter the cover permanently or you just want a temporary cover, you can make a fabric book cover or book jacket for it and decorate that instead. You can also add a simple bookplate as I did at right. I'd caution you against adding anything permanent to the cover until you're finished art journaling in it. There is often a mess out on the table while journaling, and the last thing I'm sure any of us want is to spend time creating something on the cover and then accidentally set it in a puddle of paint!

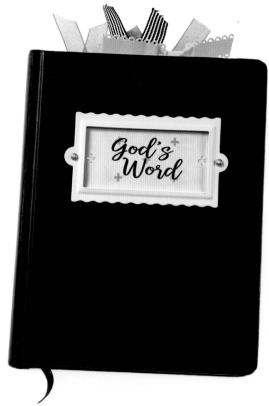

Dedication and Extra Bible Pages

Just about every Bible has a dedication page at the beginning of it, and there are many ways you can customize it.

- If you want to keep it simple, you can use stickers, stamps, or a pen to write out your name, or add a bookplate if you want it to be a bit more decorated.

- Add a prayer.

- Journaling what you hope the effect of this Bible art journal will have on your life is a great way to create focus when you begin your Bible art journal.

- Write out your life verse (your "go-to" verse for inspiration and direction) or another meaningful verse.

- Your Bible likely has extra pages of maps, concordances, and whatnot created by the publishing company to help readers. These are not the Word of God and are therefore a good place to art journal—especially when that margin just isn't enough space. Record answers to prayers, prayer requests, verses you've memorized, and more on these pages.

Faith Journaling outside of Your Bible

A natural progression for many Bible art journalers is to take art about their faith off the page. Here are some ideas you may want to try.

- Create word art of a meaningful verse, maybe one you're trying to memorize. Frame it when it's finished so you will see it and be reminded of the Word of God.

- Start a separate art journal exclusively for journaling about God's Word and your faith.

- Incorporate "faithbooking" into your scrapbooking or memory keeping. Faithbooking is just a spin-off word I use to describe scrapbook pages about my faith.

- Grab a canvas and create a larger, more detailed art piece inspired by a passage of scripture you studied and art journaled about.

- Art journal on a wide wood or plastic bangle.

- If you sew, create a fabric art piece, tote bag, or a quilt about God's Word.

Journaling on the Go

My husband travels for work often and has a "go bag" that's always packed up, ready to grab and carry out the door. If you're planning on taking your art journaling Bible on the road or over to a friend's house, you may want to gather a small stash of supplies and keep them in a small tote to carry with you. If you have a craft room packed full of art journaling supplies, don't try to take all of it with you. Think about what you actually use the most when you art journal and refer to the section in this book about must-have materials for Bible art journaling (see page 15). Many journalers worry that they won't have exactly what they need if they art journal outside their normal space. Instead of being stressed about it, look at it as a challenge to use what you have and to keep your focus on what is most important in Bible art journaling: what He is showing you in His Word and glorifying Him with the abilities He has given you as you worship Him in your artwork.

PSALM 104:34

617

Techniques and Projects

This section is a peek into my own Bible art journal. In it, I share how God motivated me to create the pages, my thought processes, which supplies I used, and step-by-step instructions on how I created them. I hope these designs inspire you to seek His Word and His guidance for your own pages. My way of creating a page isn't the "right way" or the only way it can be done. Trust that His Word is true, and that He loves you and wants you to know it and Him intimately. He will guide you if you ask Him to. Also, keep in mind that what happens in your Bible is between you and God, so be real with Him and don't create artwork with the fear of other people's judgment.

light

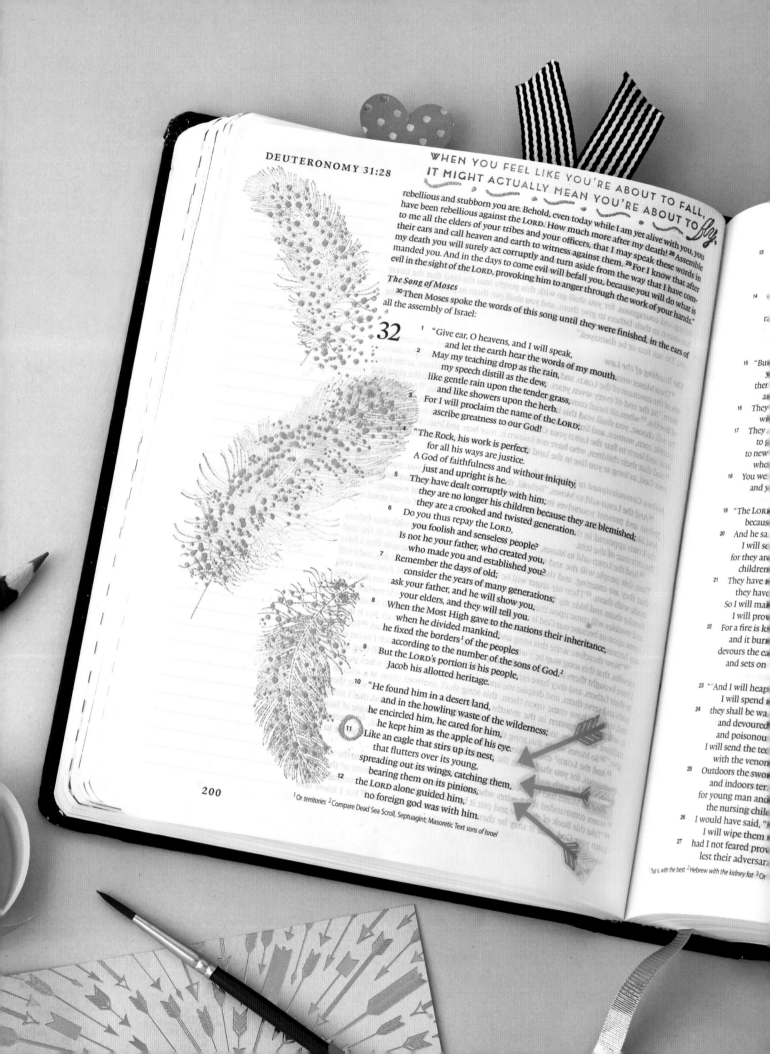

WHEN YOU FEEL LIKE YOU'RE ABOUT TO FALL, IT MIGHT ACTUALLY MEAN YOU'RE ABOUT TO *fly.*

rebellious and stubborn you are. Behold, even today while I am yet alive with you, you have been rebellious against the LORD. How much more after my death! [28] Assemble to me all the elders of your tribes and your officers, that I may speak these words in their ears and call heaven and earth to witness against them. [29] For I know that after my death you will surely act corruptly and turn aside from the way that I have commanded you. And in the days to come evil will befall you, because you will do what is evil in the sight of the LORD, provoking him to anger through the work of your hands."

The Song of Moses

[30] Then Moses spoke the words of this song until they were finished, in the ears of all the assembly of Israel:

32

[1] "Give ear, O heavens, and I will speak,
   and let the earth hear the words of my mouth.
[2] May my teaching drop as the rain,
   my speech distill as the dew,
like gentle rain upon the tender grass,
   and like showers upon the herb.
[3] For I will proclaim the name of the LORD;
   ascribe greatness to our God!

[4] "The Rock, his work is perfect,
   for all his ways are justice.
A God of faithfulness and without iniquity,
   just and upright is he.
[5] They have dealt corruptly with him;
   they are no longer his children because they are blemished;
   they are a crooked and twisted generation.
[6] Do you thus repay the LORD,
   you foolish and senseless people?
Is not he your father, who created you,
   who made you and established you?
[7] Remember the days of old;
   consider the years of many generations;
ask your father, and he will show you,
   your elders, and they will tell you.
[8] When the Most High gave to the nations their inheritance,
   when he divided mankind,
he fixed the borders[1] of the peoples
   according to the number of the sons of God.[2]
[9] But the LORD's portion is his people,
   Jacob his allotted heritage.

[10] "He found him in a desert land,
   and in the howling waste of the wilderness;
he encircled him, he cared for him,
   he kept him as the apple of his eye.
[11] Like an eagle that stirs up its nest,
   that flutters over its young,
spreading out its wings, catching them,
   bearing them on its pinions,
[12] the LORD alone guided him,
   no foreign god was with him.

[1] Or territories [2] Compare Dead Sea Scroll, Septuagint; Masoretic Text sons of Israel

200

Stamping *and* Embossing

DEUTERONOMY 32:11

While I would love to say that every Bible page I create is inspired by deep spiritual reflection, the truth is that sometimes they're inspired by an awesome new craft supply! I'm always on the lookout for materials to add to my collection of creative tools, but to keep myself in check I look for supplies that I can use for multiple purposes, like these feather stamps. In addition to using them on Bible pages, I've incorporated them into greeting cards and other crafts. They can be used for a variety of themes, such as birds, flight, writing, and lightness, or have cultural significance as in Native American culture.

When I came across this stamp collection, I did a word search in my favorite Bible app, YouVersion, for words that could tie in with these lovely feathers. I looked for words such as *birds, wings,* and *fly* until I found a verse that spoke to me and inspired me to create. I used the wet-embossing technique, in which you apply embossing ink to a stamp, then use a heat gun to adhere embossing powder to the stamped design. It creates a slightly raised design, which really pops off the page, especially when you use a metallic powder like I did here.

SUPPLIES

Feather and text stamps: *Papertrey Ink "Feather Finery"*

Acrylic blocks (that fit the stamps)

Ink: *ClearSnap ColorBox Petal Point Pigment Options Pad* in aurora

Embossing ink: *Tsukineko VersaMark*

Embossing powder: *Ranger* in princess gold

Scratch paper

Craft heat gun

Embossing pen: *Zig Emboss Writer*

Arrow stickers: *Paper Studio*

Stampin' Up! Embossing Buddy (optional if using a different brand of embossing powder)

TECHNIQUES

Stamping

Embossing

Doodling

1 Apply one of the feather stamps to an acrylic block and then place it onto your table stamp side up.

2 Pounce colored ink onto the stamp until it's completely covered.

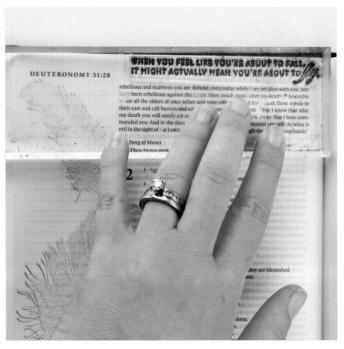

3 Pressing down firmly and evenly, stamp the feather onto the margin of your Bible.

4 Repeat Steps 1–3 with the other feather and the text stamp from the kit and allow the ink to dry.

TIP
After you tip the excess embossing powder onto the scratch paper, you can bend the paper in half to funnel the powder back into its jar to use again.

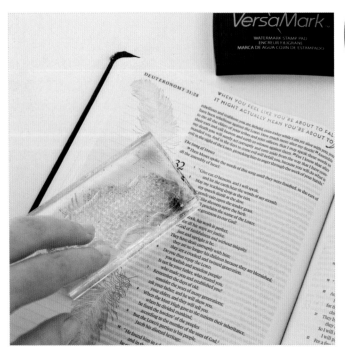

5 If you use a different brand of embossing powder, you can rub the Embossing Buddy over the page before stamping to prevent stray powder from sticking to the page. Apply the feather dots stamp to the acrylic block and then apply the embossing ink to it as you applied the color ink in Step 2. Stamp it on top of the feathers.

6 While the embossing ink is wet, sprinkle the gold embossing powder onto it, covering the embossing ink completely. Hold your Bible up vertically and gently shake off the extra embossing powder onto scratch paper.

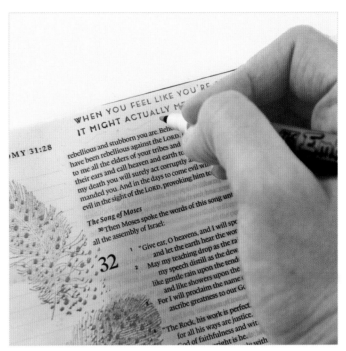

7 Turn the heat gun on and, from a distance of about 8–10" (20–25 cm), away apply the heat to the embossing powder on your Bible page. Keep the heat gun moving so it doesn't burn your pages. It should quickly melt the embossing powder, leaving a nice raised gold design. Allow it to cool before touching it.

8 Using the embossing pen, doodle under the text with a horizontal squiggle-dot-squiggle pattern and circle the verse number.

9 Apply the embossing powder to those areas, tap off the extra embossing powder onto the scratch paper, and then heat it with the heat gun.

10 Add three gold arrow stickers so they are pointing at the verse.

Doodling

EPHESIANS 4:4–6

It's no secret that I love to doodle. If I have any free time, I'm likely to be found with a pencil and notebook in hand, sketching away. That wasn't always the case. Sure, I doodled daisies and hearts on my paper-bag book covers as a kid, but I never really ventured beyond that. Why? I was afraid. What if it didn't turn out the way I planned? What if someone saw it and thought it was horrible? Thankfully, as I got older, God convicted me for not trying something He was drawing me to do. I knew that He is my Creator, and that He created me in His image (Genesis 1:27), but if I really believed that was true, why wasn't I living it? So I picked up a pencil and an old notebook and started doodling small, easy things at first and then blossomed from there by practicing, practicing, practicing.

If you're afraid to pick up that pencil, you're not alone, but our Creator made you in His image, too. You're a creative individual. So pick up a pencil and see whether this is the creative pursuit He intends for you. This page is a great way to begin doodling if you haven't done much before.

In addition to a colorful doodled design, I used letter stickers to call out the key words in this passage from Ephesians. I chose sticker colors that complement the colors in my doodle.

SUPPLIES

Letter stickers: *Lily Bee* and *Simple Stories*

Ruler

Number 1 template on page 147 (optional)

Light box or tablet device with light box app (optional)

Pencil

Eraser

Scratch paper

Black pen: *Faber-Castell PITT Artist Pen* (extra-small nib)

Colored pencils: *Prismacolor Premier* in Parma violet, canary yellow, Spanish orange, pale vermillion, blush pink, process red, carmine red, crimson red, aquamarine, grass green, and spring green

TECHNIQUES

Letter stickers

Doodling

Colored pencils

Placing Letter Stickers

To make sure your letter stickers are straight, place just the lower portion of each letter onto the edge of a clear ruler, such as the Pro Centering Craft Ruler, as shown here. When all of the letters in a word are on the ruler, place it onto your page and press on the letters as you remove the ruler.

and length and height and depth, [19] and to know the love of Christ that surpasses knowledge, that you may be filled with all the fullness of God.

[20] Now to him who is able to do far more abundantly than all that we ask or think, according to the power at work within us, [21] to him be glory in the church and in Christ Jesus throughout all generations, forever and ever. Amen.

Unity in the Body of Christ

4 I therefore, a prisoner for the Lord, urge you to walk in a manner worthy of the calling to which you have been called, [2] with all humility and gentleness, with patience, bearing with one another in love, [3] eager to maintain the unity of the Spirit in the bond of peace. [4] There is one body and one Spirit—just as you were called to the one hope that belongs to your call— [5] one Lord, one faith, one baptism, [6] one God and Father of all, who is over all and through all and in all. [7] But grace was given to each one of us according to the measure of Christ's gift. [8] Therefore it says,

a "When he ascended on high he led a host of captives,
and he gave gifts to men."[1]

[9] (In saying, "He ascended," what does it mean but that he had also descended into the lower regions, the earth?[2] [10] He who descended is the one who also ascended far above all the heavens, that he might fill all things.) [11] And he gave the apostles, the prophets, the evangelists, the shepherds[3] and teachers,[4] [12] to equip the saints for the work of ministry, for building up the body of Christ, [13] until we all attain to the unity of the faith and of the knowledge of the Son of God, to mature manhood,[5] to the measure of the stature of the fullness of Christ, [14] so that we may no longer be children, tossed to and fro by the waves and carried about by every wind of doctrine, by human cunning, by craftiness in deceitful schemes. [15] Rather, speaking the truth in love, we are to grow up in every way into him who is the head, into Christ, [16] from whom the whole body, joined and held together by every joint with which it is equipped, when each part is working properly, makes the body grow so that it builds itself up in love.

The New Life

[17] Now this I say and testify in the Lord, that you must no longer walk as the Gentiles do, in the futility of their minds. [18] They are darkened in their understanding, alienated from the life of God because of the ignorance that is in them, due to their hardness of heart. [19] They have become callous and have given themselves up to sensuality, greedy to practice every kind of impurity. [20] But that is not the way you learned Christ!— [21] assuming that you have heard about him and were taught in him, as the truth is in Jesus, [22] to put off your old self,[6] which belongs to your former manner of life and is corrupt through deceitful desires, [23] and to be renewed in the spirit of your minds, [24] and to put on the new self, created after the likeness of God in true righteousness and holiness.

[25] Therefore, having put away falsehood, let each one of you speak the truth with his neighbor, for we are members one of another. [26] Be angry and do not sin; do not let the sun go down on your anger, [27] and give no opportunity to the devil. [28] Let the thief no longer steal, but rather let him labor, doing honest work with his own hands, so that he may have something to share with anyone in need. [29] Let no corrupting talk come out of your mouths, but only such as is good for building up, as fits the occasion, that it may give grace to those who hear. [30] And do not grieve the Holy Spirit of God, by whom you were sealed for the day of redemption. [31] Let all bitterness and wrath and anger and clamor and slander be put away from you, along with all malice. [32] Be kind to one another, tenderhearted, forgiving one another, as God in Christ forgave you.

[1] The Greek word anthropoi can refer to both men and women [2] Or the lower parts of the earth? [3] Or pastors [4] Or the shepherd-teachers [5] Greek to a full-grown man [6] Greek man; also verse 24 a Ps. 68:18

1
body
SPIRIT
hope
LORD
FAITH
baptism
GOD

1263

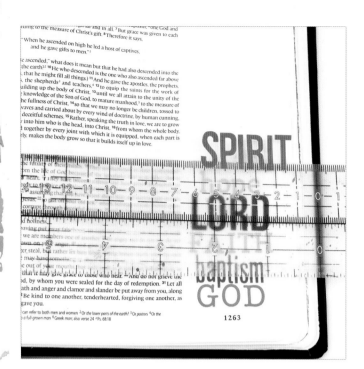

1 Apply the letter stickers to the Bible margin beginning from the bottom and working your way up. Use the ruler to help you align the stickers (see the sidebar on page 38).

2 Use a pencil to sketch out a number 1 above the sticker text or trace the template on page 147.

3 Practice making simple flowers on a scratch piece of paper and then when you're comfortable, sketch the flowers into the number 1 in your Bible. See page 27 for tips on drawing flowers.

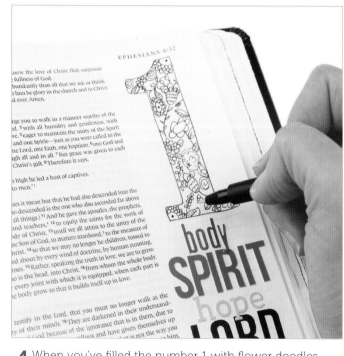

4 When you've filled the number 1 with flower doodles, trace over the pencil sketches with the black pen.

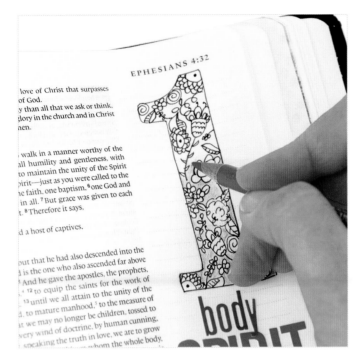

5 Color in the background of the number 1 with the aquamarine colored pencil.

6 Color in the flowers and leaves with a variety of colored pencils.

7 Using the canary yellow colored pencil, highlight the portions of the verses that state "one body . . . one Spirit . . . one hope . . . one Lord . . . one faith . . . one baptism . . . one God." Use the aquamarine colored pencil to highlight the other portions of those verses.

8 With the black pen, draw rectangles around the yellow highlighted words.

your own eye? [4] Or how can you say to your brother, 'Let me take the speck out of your eye,' when there is the log in your own eye? [5] You hypocrite, first take the log out of your own eye, and then you will see clearly to take the speck out of your brother's eye. [6] "Do not give dogs what is holy, and do not throw your pearls before pigs, lest they trample them underfoot and turn to attack you.

Ask, and It Will Be Given

[7] [a] "Ask, and it will be given to you; seek, and you will find; knock, and it will be opened to you. [8] For everyone who asks receives, and the one who seeks finds, and to the one who knocks it will be opened. [9] Or which one of you, if his son asks him for bread, will give him a stone? [10] Or if he asks for a fish, will give him a serpent? [11] If you then, who are evil, know how to give good gifts to your children, how much more will your Father who is in heaven give good things to those who ask him!

The Golden Rule

[12] "So whatever you wish that others would do to you, do also to them, for this is the Law and the Prophets.

[13] "Enter by the narrow gate. For the gate is wide and the way is easy[1] that leads to destruction, and those who enter by it are many. [14] For the gate is narrow and the way is hard that leads to life, and those who find it are few.

A Tree and Its Fruit

[15] "Beware of false prophets, who come to you in sheep's clothing but inwardly are ravenous wolves. [16] You will recognize them by their fruits. Are grapes gathered from thornbushes, or figs from thistles? [17] So, every healthy tree bears good fruit, but the diseased tree bears bad fruit. [18] A healthy tree cannot bear bad fruit, nor can a diseased tree bear good fruit. [19] Every tree that does not bear good fruit is cut down and thrown into the fire. [20] Thus you will recognize them by their fruits.

I Never Knew You

[21] "Not everyone who says to me, 'Lord, Lord,' will enter the kingdom of heaven, but the one who does the will of my Father who is in heaven. [22] On that day many will say to me, 'Lord, Lord, did we not prophesy in your name, and cast out demons in your name, and do many mighty works in your name?' [23] And then will I declare to them, 'I never knew you; depart from me, you workers of lawlessness.'

Build Your House on the Rock

[24] [b] "Everyone then who hears these words of mine and does them will be like a wise man who built his house on the rock. [25] And the rain fell, and the floods came, and the winds blew and beat on that house, but it did not fall, because it had been founded on the rock. [26] And everyone who hears these words of mine and does not do them will be like a foolish man who built his house on the sand. [27] And the rain fell, and the floods came, and the winds blew and beat against that house, and it fell, and great was the fall of it."

The Authority of Jesus

[28] And when Jesus finished these sayings, the crowds were astonished at his teaching, [29] for he was teaching them as one who had authority, and not as their scribes.

Jesus Cleanses a Leper

8 When he came down from the mountain, great crowds followed him. [2] And behold, a leper[2] came to him and knelt before him, saying, "Lord, if you will, you can make me clean." [3] And Jesus[3] stretched out his hand and touched him, saying, "I will; be clean."

[1] Some manuscripts For the way is wide and easy [2] Leprosy was a term for several skin diseases; see Leviticus 13 [3] Greek he
[a] For 7:7-11 see parallel Luke 11:9-13. [b] For 7:24-27 see parallel Luke 6:47-49. [c] For 8:2-4 see parallels Mark 1:40-44; Luke 5:12-14

And immediately his le
nothing to anyone, bu
commanded, for a pro

The Faith of a Centur

[5] [d] When he had en
to him, [6] "Lord, my s
said to him, "I will c
worthy to have you c
be healed. [9] For I too
one, 'Go,' and he go
this,' and he does i
followed him, "Tru
you, many will com
Jacob in the kingdo
the outer darkness
to the centurion J
servant was heale

Jesus Heals Man

[14] [b] And when
a fever. [15] He tou
him. [16] That eve
he cast out the s
what was spoke

The Cost of Fo

[18] Now whe
side. [19] And a s
go." [20] And Jes
Son of Man h
let me first go
dead to bury

Jesus Calms

[23] [c] And w
arose a grea
he was asle
[26] And he s
rebuked th
saying, "W

Jesus Hea

[28] [d] And
possesse
that way
Have yo
feeding
cast us
came o
bank i

[1] Greek b
also verse
1:29-34;
[d] For 8:28

Coloring with Crayons

MATTHEW 7: 13–14

Christ's followers believe that there is only one way to have an eternal relationship with the Father and that is through His Son, Jesus. The Bible describes it as entering through a narrow gate that few choose to go through. For these verses I wanted to depict that narrow road that I've chosen to follow. I added my own word art based on an anonymous quote to the margin as another way of thinking about the words of Matthew. Remember that you don't have to just quote scripture in your journal pages. This is your personal space to express your faith as the Lord inspires you.

I used good old basic crayons on this page. Crayons are great for a number of reasons. Almost everyone has some, they're inexpensive art supplies, they're easy to travel with, and, boy, are they fun to use! It takes me back to my days as a pre-school teacher! I colored the page so that the brightest part of the sunrise falls on the verses, Matthew 7:13–14, and the other colors of the sky radiate out from there. I wanted to include a beautiful sunrise as a way to "proclaim the excellencies of Him who called [me] out of darkness into His marvelous light," as 1 Peter 2:9 says.

SUPPLIES

Letter stickers: *Simple Stories*

Pencil

Eraser

Ruler

Black pens: *Faber-Castell PITT Artist Pen* (small and medium nibs)

Crayons: *Crayola* in scarlet, orange, yellow-orange, yellow, Granny Smith apple, forest green, timberwolf, raw sienna, tumbleweed, and sepia

Acrylic block or craft mat

Markers: *Faber-Castell Big Brush Markers* in May green and nougat

Water brush

Paper towel or baby wipe

TECHNIQUES

Letter stickers

Crayons

Painting with markers

1 Place the letter stickers onto the margin of the page as you use a pencil to sketch out the rest of the words. (See page 38 for tips on placing letter stickers.)

2 Use the black pens to trace over the words. Use the small tip for the smaller letters and the medium-size tip for the rest of them.

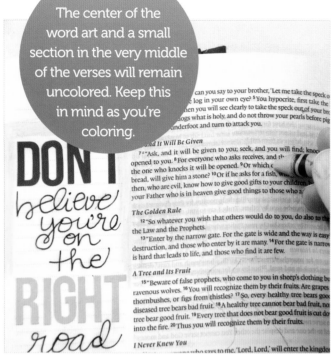

3 With a pencil, sketch the path and horizon line. The horizon line should extend to the left of the word art. Beginning at the area around the verses, color them yellow with a very, very light pressure, leaving a small amount of space in the middle of the verses uncolored so it will look like the brightest part of the design.

4 Using the same yellow crayon, apply more pressure and color about a 1" (2.5 cm) radius around the portion colored in the previous step, stopping the color at the horizon line.

5 Using an orange crayon, color on the top ¼" (6 mm) section of yellow to blend the colors together and then color about ½" (1.3 cm) above the yellow with yellow-orange. Using a red crayon, color above the area in the previous step, blending some of the two colors together.

6 Starting from the horizon line down, and using a blend of Granny Smith apple and forest green crayons, color the grass area. By using two colors, the texture of the grass is revealed. Be mindful of the direction of your strokes; you want them to be primarily going in a vertical direction, just like grass would be.

7 To color the path, use the tumbleweed crayon in the center of it and sepia toward the edges. Create some small rocks by making dots with the timberwolf colored crayon along the path.

8 On an acrylic block or craft mat, scribble with the May green marker. Use the water brush to pick up some color and paint the grass along the edge of the path. This gives the illusion of new growing grass and helps define it. When you're finished, clean the ink off your acrylic block with a wet paper towel or baby wipe and allow the ink to dry.

9 Scribble the nougat Big Brush Marker onto the acrylic block or craft mat and use the water brush to pick up some and paint it onto the edge of the path; let the ink dry.

10 Draw small dots with the May green marker onto the edge of the grass and use the nougat marker to make dots on the path. This gives it some texture.

Gelatos

PSALM 51:10

Psalm 51 describes David's repentance and God's forgiveness after he had an affair with Bathsheba and murdered her husband, Uriah. David recognizes that he was born as a sinner and that as he chose to sin, he not only wronged those who were affected by what he had done, but he also sinned against the Lord. He begged Him for forgiveness. Although I haven't had an affair or murdered anyone, I too have sinned, but because of God's unconditional love for me, I knew that when I asked Him to forgive me and come be a part of my life as my Lord that He would. That's why when I came across this verse again it really meant a great deal to me because it reminded me of when I decided to trust Him for His forgiveness and salvation.

This is a theme that speaks to my heart, so I could think of no better way to illustrate that theme than with a beautiful heart. I used a heart cutout as a mask to surround it with color. Gelatos are a wonderful medium for this purpose, as they provide luminous color that lets the words of scripture shine through.

SUPPLIES

Pencil

Eraser

Heart template (page 147)

Card stock

Scissors

Faber-Castell Gelatos in bubblegum and red cherry

Makeup sponge (optional)

Black pens: *Sakura Pigma FB Pen; Faber-Castell PITT Artist Pen* (extra-small nib)

Washi tape: *Doodlebug*

TECHNIQUES

Masking

Gelatos

Lettering

More Ideas for Working with Gelatos

Gelatos are a versatile medium that can be incorporated into your Bible art journaling in many more ways than how I used them in this project:

- Mix them with another medium, such as texture paste or gel medium, to give it color.

- Spread some Gelatos onto a palette, mix in a couple drops of water, and use the mixture as you would watercolor.

- Apply Gelatos directly to your Bible page and use a wet paintbrush to blend the color around.

- Use Gelatos in place of ink for stamping to create a distressed, "artsy" look.

- Mix Gelatos and water in a bowl and then transfer it into a plastic spray bottle to mist color onto your page.

- Use a damp makeup sponge or your finger to apply Gelatos to a stencil. (See Stenciling and Masking on page 58.)

- Gelatos can be applied to a variety of surfaces as well. Besides your Bible pages, try them on canvas, fabric, textured or patterned card stock, and watercolor paper.

The one who offers thanksgiving as his sacrifice glorifies me;
to one who orders his way rightly
I will show the salvation of God!"

Create in Me a Clean Heart, O God

To the choirmaster. A Psalm of David, when Nathan the
prophet went to him, after he had gone in to Bathsheba.

51 ¹ Have mercy on me, O God,
according to your steadfast love;
according to your abundant mercy
blot out my transgressions.
² Wash me thoroughly from my iniquity,
and cleanse me from my sin!

³ For I know my transgressions,
and my sin is ever before me.
⁴ Against you, you only, have I sinned
and done what is evil in your sight,
so that you may be justified in your words
and blameless in your judgment.
⁵ Behold, I was brought forth in iniquity,
and in sin did my mother conceive me.
⁶ Behold, you delight in truth in the inward being,
and you teach me wisdom in the secret heart.

⁷ Purge me with hyssop, and I shall be clean;
wash me, and I shall be whiter than snow.
⁸ Let me hear joy and gladness;
let the bones that you have broken rejoice.
⁹ Hide your face from my sins,
and blot out all my iniquities.
¹⁰ Create in me a clean heart, O God,
and renew a right spirit within me.
¹¹ Cast me not away from your presence,
and take not your Holy Spirit from me.
¹² Restore to me the joy of your salvation,
and uphold me with a willing spirit.

¹³ Then I will teach transgressors your ways,
and sinners will return to you.
¹⁴ Deliver me from bloodguiltiness, O God,
O God of my salvation,
and my tongue will sing aloud of your righteousness.
¹⁵ O Lord, open my lips,
and my mouth will declare your praise.
¹⁶ For you will not delight in sacrifice, or I would give it;
you will not be pleased with a burnt offering.
¹⁷ The sacrifices of God are a broken spirit;
a broken and contrite heart, O God, you will not despise.

¹⁸ Do good to Zion in your good pleasure;
build up the walls of Jerusalem;

Selah

51

create in me a clean Heart, O God, & renew a right spirit within me

TIP
Place the heart template so that it is mostly covering a blank portion of the Bible page. You will be adding text to this area.

1 Trace the heart pattern on page 147 onto a piece of card stock and cut it out. The card stock heart will be used as a mask on this page, so place it where you'd like it to go and hold it down firmly.

2 Start by directly applying the bubblegum Gelato closest to the heart.

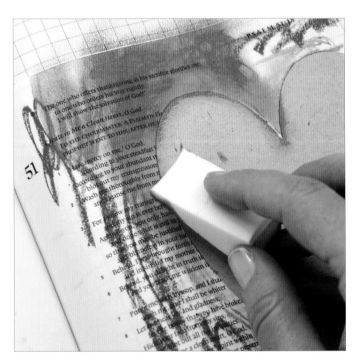

3 Add the red cherry color Gelato beyond where you colored with the bubblegum Gelato.

4 Use a makeup sponge (or your fingers) to blend and smooth out the colors. Allow the Gelatos to cure before proceeding so they don't smudge onto the masked-off heart space.

5 Using a pencil, add your word art to the center of the heart shape.

6 Trace over the thicker letters in the word art with the Sakura Pigma FB Pen.

7 Use the Faber-Castell PITT Artist Pen to trace over the thinner letters. After allowing the ink to dry, erase the pencil lines.

8 Apply pieces of washi tape to the top and bottom areas of the page.

Give Thanks to the LORD, for He Is Good

106

1 Praise the LORD!
  Oh give thanks to the LORD, for he is good,
    for his steadfast love endures forever!
2 Who can utter the mighty deeds of the LORD,
    or declare all his praise?
3 Blessed are they who observe justice,
    who do righteousness at all times!

4 Remember me, O LORD, when you show favor to your people;
    help me when you save them,¹
5 that I may look upon the prosperity of your chosen ones,
    that I may rejoice in the gladness of your nation,
    that I may glory with your inheritance.

6 Both we and our fathers have sinned;
    we have committed iniquity; we have done wickedness.
7 Our fathers, when they were in Egypt,
    did not consider your wondrous works;
  they did not remember the abundance of your steadfast love,
    but rebelled by the sea, at the Red Sea.
8 Yet he saved them for his name's sake,
    that he might make known his mighty power.
9 He rebuked the Red Sea, and it became dry,
    and he led them through the deep as through a desert.
10 So he saved them from the hand of the foe
    and redeemed them from the power of the enemy.
11 And the waters covered their adversaries;
    not one of them was left.
12 Then they believed his words;
    they sang his praise.

13 But they soon forgot his works;
    they did not wait for his counsel.
14 But they had a wanton craving in the wilderness,
    and put God to the test in the desert;
15 he gave them what they asked,
    but sent a wasting disease among them.

16 When men in the camp were jealous of Moses
    and Aaron, the holy one of the LORD,
17 the earth opened and swallowed up Dathan,
    and covered the company of Abiram.
18 Fire also broke out in their company;
    the flame burned up the wicked.

19 They made a calf in Horeb
    and worshiped a metal image.
20 They exchanged the glory of God²
    for the image of an ox that eats grass.
21 They forgot God, their Savior,
    who had done great things in Egypt,

¹ Or Remember me, O LORD, with the favor you show to your people; help me with your salvation   ² Hebrew exchanged their glory

620

O THANKFUL Lord, you good and true of love are always for us.

Stamping with Distress Inks

PSALM 106:1–2

One Thanksgiving when I was searching the Bible for scriptures that I could use in another holiday art project, I came across Psalm 106:1–2. These verses talk about God's goodness, unchanging love, and all the great acts He does that we can't ever praise enough. Just reading them provoked such gratefulness for Him that I knew I wanted to create a page based on it.

I decided to use Distress Inks for this page because they come in so many great fall colors that are really versatile for mixing, matching, and layering over one another. Although there are many ways to use Distress Inks, one of my go-to techniques is just to blend them with an Ink Blending Tool. These tools have a foam pad that attaches onto the end of it so you can use a new foam color for each shade of Distress Ink you're using. (I like to keep each of the foams underneath each color of ink for future use so I don't waste them.)

Using stamps with the ink-blending technique is great if you're intimidated by drawing your own designs or if you just really love a certain stamp and want to use it on your page.

SUPPLIES

Acrylic blocks or *MISTI*

Stamps: *Papertrey Ink "Thankful for You"*

Scratch paper

Ink: *Ranger Distress Ink* in carved pumpkin, crushed olive, brushed corduroy, walnut stain, mustard seed, scattered straw, and antique linen

Ink applicator: *Ranger Distress Ink Blending Tool and Foam*

Pens: *Staedtler Triplus Fineliner* in brown; *PITT Artist Pen* in cold grey (brush nib)

Colored pencil: *Prismacolor Premier* in light umber

TECHNIQUES

Stamping

Ink blending

Stamping with the MISTI

Acrylic stamps need to be placed on some type of block in order to stamp with them. Using an acrylic block made for stamping is the most common method. But when you are using multiple stamps in a design, it can be difficult to arrange them exactly as you want them to appear on your Bible page. And once you stamp, it's too late to rearrange them. The MISTI, the Most Incredible Stamp Tool Invented, is a precision stamp tool that takes the guesswork out of stamping. The other advantage of the MISTI is that if your image doesn't stamp correctly the first time, you can re-ink it and restamp in the exact same spot. Follow Steps 1–5 to use the MISTI.

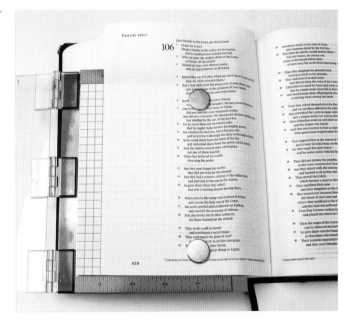

1 If using the MISTI, place the pad section under the Bible page, making sure it's straight before anchoring it with the magnets. If using acrylic blocks, skip to Step 3.

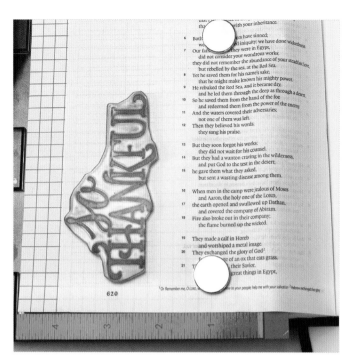

2 Place the "so thankful" stamp onto the page where you want it to go.

3 Close the acrylic plate over the stamp. If you're using acrylic blocks instead of the MISTI, place the stamp onto the block.

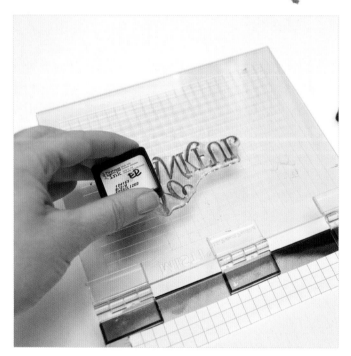

4 Ink the stamp starting with yellow in the middle, then orange to the left of it, green to the right, and brown at both ends.

5 Close the MISTI or use the acrylic block to stamp the words onto the page.

6 Place the wheat and leaf stamps on acrylic blocks and, with various ink colors, stamp around the page.

7 With a piece of scratch paper under your page, apply light brown ink to a Distress Ink Blending Tool's foam and use a light swirling motion to ink the edges of the page.

8 Use a brown pen to journal a prayer under "so thankful" so that the words float around the leaves. With the brown pen, add small dots around the edges of the page.

9 Use the gray pen to add delicate shadows around the stamped words and leaves.

10 With a brown colored pencil, draw subtle veins on the stamped leaves.

LIVE
How to
what to
DO 6

> "The LORD has shown you what is good. He has told you what he requires of you. You must treat people fairly. You must love others faithfully. And you must be very careful to live the way your God wants you to."
> Micah 6:8

always ✝✝

10 And in that day, declares the LORD,
I will cut off your horses from among you
and will destroy your chariots;
11 and I will cut off the cities of your land
and throw down all your strongholds;
12 and I will cut off sorceries from your hand,
and you shall have no more tellers of fortunes;
13 and I will cut off your carved images
and your pillars from among you,
and you shall bow down no more
to the work of your hands;
14 and I will root out your Asherah images from among you
and destroy your cities.
15 And in anger and wrath I will execute vengeance
on the nations that did not obey.

The Indictment of the LORD

1 Hear what the LORD says:
Arise, plead your case before the mountains,
and let the hills hear your voice.
2 Hear, you mountains, the indictment of the LORD,
and you enduring foundations of the earth,
for the LORD has an indictment against his people,
and he will contend with Israel.

3 "O my people, what have I done to you?
How have I wearied you? Answer me!
4 For I brought you up from the land of Egypt
and redeemed you from the house of slavery,
and I sent before you Moses,
Aaron, and Miriam.
5 O my people, remember what Balak king of Moab devised,
and what Balaam the son of Beor answered him,
and what happened from Shittim to Gilgal,
that you may know the righteous acts of the LORD."

What Does the LORD Require?

6 With what shall I come before the LORD,
and bow myself before God on high?
Shall I come before him with burnt offerings,
with calves a year old?
7 Will the LORD be pleased with¹ thousands of rams,
with ten thousands of rivers of oil?
Shall I give my firstborn for my transgression,
the fruit of my body for the sin of my soul?"
8 He has told you, O man, what is good;
and what does the LORD require of you
but to do justice, and to love kindness,²
and to walk humbly with your God?

Destruction of the Wicked

9 The voice of the LORD cries to the city—
and it is sound wisdom to fear your name:

¹ Or the LORD accept, ² Or steadfast love

Using Journaling Kits

Although I love, love, love to create my own artwork for my Bible, there are some wonderful premade products out there. Kits are a great place to start if you're intimidated about trying Bible journaling or if you're unsure how to combine embellishments. They are a help when you want to record what's in your heart but you don't have a lot of time.

Keep in mind that purchased kits may use a different version of the Bible than you are using for your art journaling. If you feel strongly about which version you use, always double-check the verses before you buy. I enjoy reading a couple of different trusted versions because they round out my understanding of the scripture, so it's not often an issue for me.

This page features a well-known Bible verse, Micah 6:8. The verse breaks down how we are to live a life that pleases the Lord: do justice, love kindness, and walk humbly with the Lord. I wanted to add some thoughts on these verses, and because there isn't a lot of space, I used a premade card and some washi tape to create a tip-in that can be lifted up to reveal my thoughts on this scripture.

Custom Letter Stamping

Letter stamps are a fun and easy way to add lettering to your Bible page. There are hundreds of wonderful stamps available, some made specifically for Bible journaling and others for general crafting. But just because you're using purchased stamps doesn't mean you can't add your own personal touch.

- Mix and match different styles and sizes.
- Instead of ink, color them with markers, watercolors, or Gelatos.
- After stamping, add your own doodles with contrasting pens, as in this project. Stripes, dots, and dashes are easy additions that create a lot of impact. If the stamps are large enough you can try more elaborate doodles, such as flowers.
- Combine letter stamps and your own hand lettering.

SUPPLIES

Washi tape: *Documented Faith "Doodle Scallop"; Doodlebug "Beetle Black Swiss Dot"*

Markers: *Faber-Castell Big Brush Markers* in pink madder lake, cobalt green, and cobalt blue

Sticker tape: *Documented Faith "Teach Kit"*

Stamps: *Documented Faith "Doodle Alpha"*

Acrylic stamp block or *MISTI*

Chalk ink: *Quick Quotes Powder Puff Chalking Ink* in midnight confession

Colored pencils: *Prismacolor Premier* in peacock blue, process red, Parma violet, olive green, and metallic silver

Black pen: *Faber-Castell PITT Artist Pen* (medium nib)

White gel pen: *Signo*

Adhesive: *Scotch Advanced Tape Glider* (ATG)

Tabs: *Documented Faith "Teach Kit"*

Stapler: *Ranger Tiny Attacher*

Ribbon: *May Arts*

Sticker: *Documented Faith Word Strips "Icons"*

Card: *Documented Faith "Teach Kit"*

TECHNIQUES

Stamping

Markers

Colored pencils

Creating a tip-in

Creating a bookmark

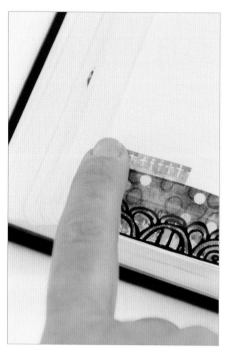

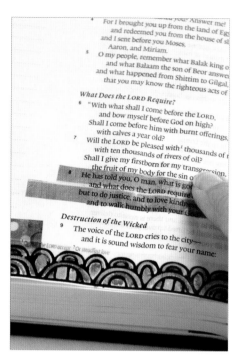

1 Rip off a piece of the scalloped washi tape that is the same size as the width of the page and apply it to the bottom of it. Using the various marker colors, color in the washi tape.

2 Apply a piece of the green dot sticker tape that is the size of the page margin above the left side of the longer washi tape, overlapping slightly. Add a 1½" (3.8 cm) piece of pink cross sticker tape above the washi tape.

3 Apply two pieces of blue washi tape to cover the verse Micah 6:8. The words will still be visible.

4 Apply the letters on the stamp block or MISTI to spell out "live" and "do." Ink it with chalk ink and stamp it onto the upper margin of the page. (See page 51 for instructions on using the MISTI.)

5 Use a black pen to write "how to" above "live" and "what to" above "do." Color the letters using colored pencils. Use a black and a white pen to doodle onto the letters. Add stripes, dots, and other designs to the letters to give them a fun, one-of-a-kind look.

6 To make a bookmark, apply ATG adhesive to a tab and place it at the top of the page, folding it over to adhere it to both sides. Use a stapler to attach a small piece of ribbon to the tab. Add the sticker that says "always" to the tab.

7 Place the sticker with a verse on it in the center of the card.

8 Apply adhesive to the back of a tab and then adhere it to the right side, center edge, of the card.

9 Rip off a piece of washi tape the same length as the card and adhere half of it to the card. Place the card on the left side of the page, then wrap the remaining washi tape onto the back of the page.

10 If desired, journal personal thoughts or quotes in the space behind the card.

Stenciling and Masking

ACTS 4:12

While driving in my car one day, the song "No Other Name" by Hillsong United came on. As I sang along worshiping the Lord, I really focused on the lyrics of the song. They were still running through my head hours later, so I decided to create a page about the meaning of the song in my Bible art journal using the verse Acts 4:12.

I chose this verse because it talks about how it's only through Jesus that we can be saved from the penalty of being a sinful human being; God hasn't provided the world any other alternative for salvation. Reading that reminded me that He is my King of Kings and above all, so I decided to use purple, the color of royalty, as the predominant color.

This page features two ways to stencil: I used a traditional stencil with a design reminiscent of crosses and also "reverse stenciling," or masking, using letter stickers that spell "Jesus" to create a bold focal point.

SUPPLIES

Letter stickers: *American Crafts Remarks "Smokey Joes"*

Faber-Castell Gelatos in raspberry and metallic grape

Palette paper

Stencil: *Prima Marketing "Lattice"*

Makeup sponge (optional)

Baby wipes or wet paper towels

Colored pencils: *Prismacolor Premier* in Parma violet and sienna brown

Pencil

Eraser

Markers: *Tombow Dual Brush Pens* in #665 (dark purple) and #606 (light purple)

TECHNIQUES

Stenciling

Masking

Gelatos

Letter stickers

Lettering

1 Apply letter stickers to the margin of the Bible starting from the bottom of the page; place the end of the word (S) and continue to add the remaining letters up the page, ending with the first letter (J).

TIP
If your stickers are really sticky, tap them on your clothing to gather some lint and avoid damaging your page when you remove them.

him this man is standing before you well. [11] This Jesus[1] is the stone that was rejected by you, the builders, which has become the cornerstone.[2] [12] And there is salvation in no one else, for there is no other name under heaven given among men[3] by which we must be saved."

[13] Now when they saw the boldness of Peter and John, and perceived that they were uneducated, common men, they were astonished. And they recognized that they had been with Jesus. [14] But seeing the man who was healed standing beside them, they had nothing to say in opposition. [15] But when they had commanded them to leave the council, they conferred with one another, [16] saying, "What shall we do with these men? For that a notable sign has been performed through them is evident to all the inhabitants of Jerusalem, and we cannot deny it. [17] But in order that it may spread no further among the people, let us warn them to speak no more to anyone in this name." [18] So they called them and charged them not to speak or teach at all in the name of Jesus. [19] But Peter and John answered them, "Whether it is right in the sight of God to listen to you rather than to God, you must judge, [20] for we cannot but speak of what we have seen and heard." [21] And when they had further threatened them, they let them go, finding no way to punish them, because of the people, for all were praising God for what had happened. [22] For the man on whom this sign of healing was performed was more than forty years old.

The Believers Pray for Boldness

[23] When they were released, they went to their friends and reported what the chief priests and the elders had said to them. [24] And when they heard it, they lifted their voices together to God and said, "Sovereign Lord, who made the heaven and the earth and the sea and everything in them, [25] who through the mouth of our father David, your servant,[4] said by the Holy Spirit,

> "'Why did the Gentiles rage,
>   and the peoples plot in vain?
> [26] The kings of the earth set themselves,
>   and the rulers were gathered together,
>   against the Lord and against his Anointed'[5]—

[27] for truly in this city there were gathered together against your holy servant Jesus, whom you anointed, both Herod and Pontius Pilate, along with the Gentiles and the peoples of Israel, [28] to do whatever your hand and your plan had predestined to take place. [29] And now, Lord, look upon their threats and grant to your servants[6] to continue to speak your word with all boldness, [30] while you stretch out your hand to heal, and signs and wonders are performed through the name of your holy servant Jesus." [31] And when they had prayed, the place in which they were gathered together was shaken, and they were all filled with the Holy Spirit and continued to speak the word of God with boldness.

They Had Everything in Common

[32] Now the full number of those who believed were of one heart and soul, and no one said that any of the things that belonged to him was his own, but they had everything in common. [33] And with great power the apostles were giving their testimony to the resurrection of the Lord Jesus, and great grace was upon them all. [34] There was not a needy person among them, for as many as were owners of lands or houses sold them and brought the proceeds of what was sold [35] and laid it at the apostles' feet, and it was distributed to each as any had need. [36] Thus Joseph, who was also called by the apostles Barnabas (which means son of encouragement), a Levite, a native of Cyprus, [37] sold a field that belonged to him and brought the money and laid it at the apostles' feet.

[1] Greek This one [2] Greek the head of the corner [3] The Greek word anthropoi refers here to both men and women [4] Or child; also verses 27, 30 [5] Or Christ [6] Greek bondservants [a] Ps. 2:1, 2

NO
other
name
than

JESUS

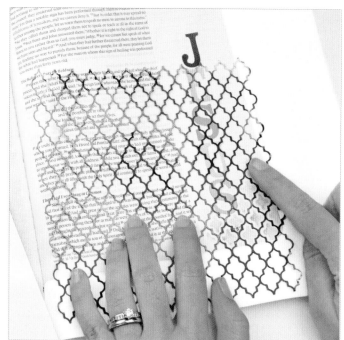

2 Apply a generous amount of each color of Gelato to the palette paper.

3 Place the stencil over the page, dab your finger (or a makeup sponge) onto a baby wipe or wet paper towel, then rub it into one color of Gelato. Working in a small section, rub the Gelato gently in a circular motion over the stencil. Alternating colors, color the rest of the page, leaving the letter stickers and the area above them un-stenciled.

4 Remove the stencil, pick up more of the Gelatos onto your finger, then rub them along the edges of the page and over the letter stickers.

5 Gently remove the letter stickers, taking care not to tear your Bible page.

6 Outline the letters and underline the verse (Acts 4:12) with the Parma violet colored pencil.

7 Using a pencil, sketch the words "No other name than" into the margin space above the word "Jesus."

8 Using the fine-tip side of the light purple marker, trace over the word art. Use the fine tip of the dark purple marker to add small polka dots to the letters.

9 Use the sienna brown colored pencil to color the cross, and then erase any remaining pencil sketch lines.

THE FIRST LETTER OF JOHN

1 JOHN

The Word of Life

1 That which was from the beginning, which we have heard, which we have seen with our eyes, which we looked upon and have touched with our hands, concerning the word of life— [2] the life was made manifest, and we have seen it, and testify to it and proclaim to you the eternal life, which was with the Father and was made manifest to us— [3] that which we have seen and heard we proclaim also to you, so that you too may have fellowship with us; and indeed our fellowship is with the Father and with his Son Jesus Christ. [4] And we are writing these things so that our[1] joy may be complete.

Walking in the Light

[5] This is the message we have heard from him and proclaim to you, that God is light, and in him is no darkness at all. [6] If we say we have fellowship with him while we walk in darkness, we lie and do not practice the truth. [7] But if we walk in the light, as he is in the light, we have fellowship with one another, and the blood of Jesus his Son cleanses us from all sin. [8] If we say we have no sin, we deceive ourselves, and the truth is not in us. [9] If we confess our sins, he is faithful and just to forgive us our sins and to cleanse us from all unrighteousness. [10] If we say we have not sinned, we make him a liar, and his word is not in us.

Christ Our Advocate

2 My little children, I am writing these things to you so that you may not sin. But if anyone does sin, we have an advocate with the Father, Jesus Christ the righteous. [2] He is the propitiation for our sins, and not for ours only but also for the sins of the whole world. [3] And by this we know that we have come to know him, if we keep his commandments. [4] Whoever says "I know him" but does not keep his commandments is a liar, and the truth is not in him, [5] but whoever keeps his word, in him truly the love of God is perfected. By this we may know that we are in him: [6] whoever says he abides in him ought to walk in the same way in which he walked.

The New Commandment

[7] Beloved, I am writing you no new commandment, but an old commandment that you had from the beginning. The old commandment is the word that you have heard. [8] At the same time, it is a new commandment that I am writing to you, which is true in him and in you, because[2] the darkness is passing away and the true light is already shining. [9] Whoever says he is in the light and hates his brother is still in darkness. [10] Whoever loves his brother abides in the light, and in him[3] there is no cause for stumbling. [11] But whoever hates his brother is in the darkness and walks in the darkness, and does not know where he is going, because the darkness has blinded his eyes.

[12] I am writing to you, little children,
    because your sins are forgiven for his name's sake.
[13] I am writing to you, fathers,
    because you know him who is from the beginning.
I am writing to you, young men,
    because you have overcome the evil one.

[1] Some manuscripts your [2] Or that [3] Or it

I write to y
    becaus
[14] I write to
    becaus
I write to
    becaus
    and th
    and y

Do Not Love the World

[15] Do not love the w
love of the Father is no
and the desires of the
world. [17] And the wor
will of God abides for

Warning Concernin

[18] Children, it is t
now many antichris
went out from us, bu
continued with us.
of us. [20] But you ha
[21] I write to you, not
because no lie is of t
This is the antichri
Son has the Father.
from the beginnin
then you too will
made to us[3]—ete
[26] I write thes
anointing that y
should teach you
is no lie—just as

Children of Go

[28] And now,
confidence and
is righteous, y
born of him.

3 See what k
of God; an
not know him
appeared; bu
see him as he
[4] Everyone
ness. [5] You k
[6] No one wh
seen him or
righteousn
is of the de
of God app
a practice
because he

[1] Or pride in po

god
is
LIGHT
in
him
is no
darkness

Spray Inks

1 JOHN 1:5–10

People have always sought enlightenment. The Bible makes it clear that there is only one way to obtain that: through God's pure light. This passage from John speaks of how believers must live in the light of His truth and holiness, not in the darkness of sin.

I wanted this page to be all about the light of God, so I put my thinking cap on and considered all the ways I could represent light. Of course a light bulb was on that list, and because they are relatively easy to draw, I decided to go with that. I wanted to fill the page with light but not cover the scripture. Spray ink was the perfect medium to achieve my vision because most lighter colors are translucent.

Spray inks contain highly pigmented ink that you can use to spray, drip, or paint onto your pages. I really love them because they are easy to use and add a lot of color to the page quickly. They are also great to use in a situation like this, where I want the yellow color to gently fade out as a real light bulb's light would.

SUPPLIES

Chipboard letters: *Advantus by Heidi Swapp*

Paper towels or scratch paper

Spray ink: *Ranger Distress Spray* in squeezed lemonade

Colored pencils: *Prismacolor Premier* in Spanish orange, metallic silver, and black

Light bulb drawing (page 151; optional)

Light box or tablet device with light box app

Pencil

Black letter stickers: *Lilly Bee Designs*

TECHNIQUES

Masking

Spray inks

Colored pencils

Stickers

Drawing or tracing

Tips for Working with Spray Inks

- Because spray inks are liquid, your page may wrinkle, especially if you use a lot of it. I prefer to do a couple quick squirts about 10 inches (25 cm) above my page and I keep my hand moving over the page as I spray. The ink is misted onto the page and usually won't cause wrinkles.

- Did you use pump hair spray back in junior high? Remember how it would sometimes clog and spray in a wonky way? Yeah, that can happen with spray ink, too, especially if you have one that contains shimmer. Make sure you work on a protected surface and cover the opposite page if you don't want it sprayed. It's also a good idea to put a paper towel or scratch paper under the page you're working on so that if it does bleed through it won't affect the pages underneath it.

- Spray inks may bleed through the page, especially darker colors. For some people that's a tragedy, for others it's not a big deal. If it is going to bother you, paint a light coat of clear gesso onto the page to act as a barrier to prevent the spray ink from bleeding through.

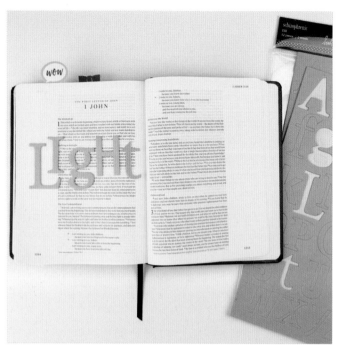

1 Place the chipboard letters down onto the center of the page. They may be covering some of the scripture, but because the yellow spray ink is a light color it will still be readable.

2 Place a paper towel or sheet of paper underneath the page you're working on. Cover the opposite page with a paper towel or sheet of paper to protect it from getting sprayed.

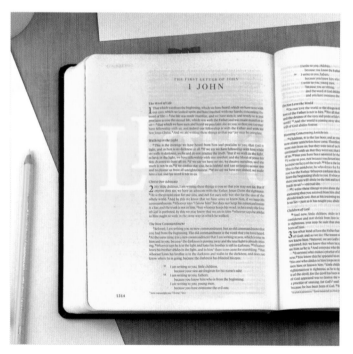

3 Hold the spray ink about 10" (25 cm) above the page and quickly spray a few pumps of spray ink, keeping your hand moving at all times to prevent big drips or puddles. Concentrate the spray ink over the letters and let it fade outward.

4 Remove the chipboard letters from the page and allow the page to dry. If there are any droplets, you can soak them up with a paper towel and then allow the page to dry.

5 Use the Spanish orange colored pencil to color around each of the letters to make them stand out a bit more.

6 Sketch a light bulb around the letters using a pencil or trace the design on page 151. Use a metallic gray colored pencil to color in the bottom of the bulb.

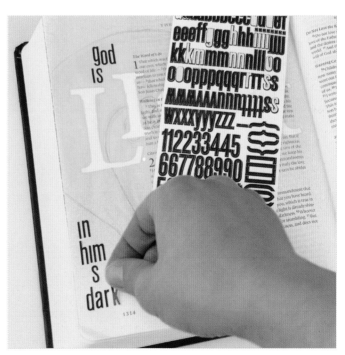

7 Trace over the pencil lines with a black colored pencil.

8 Adhere letter stickers onto the page to spell "God is" and "in him is no darkness."

Decoupage

2 PETER 3:18

Peter's final words in verses 17 and 18 talk about being on guard, growing in God's grace and knowledge, and glorifying God now and forever. What a terrific recipe for maturing and persevering in faith! With that in mind, as I prepared to start the page, I thought about how to visually represent these verses. I realized that to me the best visual reminder of growth is flowers. I cut some bunches of flowers out of a piece of tissue paper and glued them onto my page for a decoupage effect. Gel medium or decoupage medium works for this as well; just be mindful not to get your page too wet if you want to avoid wrinkling. I then decided to take the thoughts from this passage and make a little florist's card with those words on them and tuck it into the flowers on my page. Typically when decoupaging, you seal your project when you're finished, but because I didn't want my Bible page to become too thick and I don't expect it to have a lot of wear and tear I didn't seal it. If you feel like it does need sealing, apply gel medium or decoupage medium over the top of your cutouts.

SUPPLIES

Patterned tissue paper *(The Paper Studio)* or paper napkin

Fine-tip scissors: *Fiskars*

Camera (optional)

Glue stick, gel medium, or decoupage medium

Paintbrush (optional)

Ruler

Cream-colored card stock

Scalloped-edge scissors

Black pen: *Faber-Castell PITT Artist Pen* (small nib)

Pencil

Eraser

Ink applicator: *Ranger Distress Ink Blending Tool and Foam*

Ink: *Distress Ink* in antique linen

Craft mat

TECHNIQUES

Fussy cutting

Decoupage

Lettering

TIP
If you're using a paper napkin, first separate the layers. It takes a few extra minutes, but it's necessary so that the napkin is lighter and less bulky.

1 Place the tissue paper on top of the Bible page and move it around so that you can decide which patterns to cut out. As you're formulating a plan, see which designs fit well and which can be layered or cut off.

water by the word of God, [6] and that by means of these the world that then existed was deluged with water and perished. [7] But by the same word the heavens and earth that now exist are stored up for fire, being kept until the day of judgment and destruction of the ungodly.

[8] But do not overlook this one fact, beloved, that with the Lord one day is as a thousand years, and a thousand years as one day. [9] The Lord is not slow to fulfill his promise as some count slowness, but is patient toward you,[1] not wishing that any should perish, but that all should reach repentance. [10] But the day of the Lord will come like a thief, and then the heavens will pass away with a roar, and the heavenly bodies[2] will be burned up and dissolved, and the earth and the works that are done on it will be exposed.[3]

[11] Since all these things are thus to be dissolved, what sort of people ought you to be in lives of holiness and godliness, [12] waiting for and hastening the coming of the day of God, because of which the heavens will be set on fire and dissolved, and the heavenly bodies will melt as they burn! [13] But according to his promise we are waiting for new heavens and a new earth in which righteousness dwells.

Final Words

[14] Therefore, beloved, since you are waiting for these, be diligent to be found by him without spot or blemish, and at peace. [15] And count the patience of our Lord as salvation, just as our beloved brother Paul also wrote to you according to the wisdom given him, [16] as he does in all his letters when he speaks in them of these matters. There are some things in them that are hard to understand, which the ignorant and unstable twist to their own destruction, as they do the other Scriptures. [17] You therefore, beloved, knowing this beforehand, take care that you are not carried away with the error of lawless people and lose your own stability. [18] But grow in the grace and knowledge of our Lord and Savior Jesus Christ. To him be the glory both now and to the day of eternity. Amen.

GROW in grace & GLORIFY God

TIP
If you're afraid you won't remember how you had all the pieces laid out on the page, use your camera to snap a quick photo that you can refer back to.

2 Using sharp fine-tip scissors, "fussy cut" out the design. The term *fussy cutting* refers to the meticulous way you cut as close to the image as possible with scissors.

3 Arrange the images you plan to use on the page as you'd like them to be laid out. Make any necessary adjustments.

4 Place the paper pieces alongside the Bible. Working in sections, use a glue stick to adhere the tissue paper to the page. Leave an area unglued so you can add a card in a later step. If using gel medium or decoupage medium, apply it with a paintbrush to the page, lay the image on it, then paint another layer on top as you smooth it out.

5 Repeat Step 4 until all of the design is adhered and then allow it to dry. Turn the page over so that you can clearly see the edge of the Bible page. Trim off any tissue paper that hangs off the edges of the Bible page.

6 Measure the space where you want your card to go. Trim a piece of cream-colored card stock ½" (1.3 cm) larger in width and height than those dimensions. Use scalloped scissors to trim the card to the proper dimensions. Use a ruler to draw a border line around the inside of the card with a black pen.

7 Use a pencil to sketch out your text onto the card. Trace over the pencil lines with a black pen.

8 Tap a Distress Ink Applicator into Distress Ink. Starting with the applicator half on the craft mat and half on the card, use a circular rubbing motion to lightly ink the edges of the card.

9 Apply adhesive to the back of the card and tuck it under the flowers, adhering it to the page. Mark the verse by putting brackets around it with the black pen.

the *trees* of the *forest*

sing for *joy* before the *Lord*

14 He is the LORD our God;
   his judgments are in all the earth.
15 Remember his covenant forever,
   the word that he commanded, for a thousand generations,
16 the covenant that he made with Abraham,
   his sworn promise to Isaac,
17 which he confirmed to Jacob as a statute,
   to Israel as an everlasting covenant,
18 saying, "To you I will give the land of Canaan,
   as your portion for an inheritance."

19 When you were few in number,
   of little account, and sojourners in it,
20 wandering from nation to nation,
   from one kingdom to another people,
21 he allowed no one to oppress them;
   he rebuked kings on their account,
22 saying, "Touch not my anointed ones,
   do my prophets no harm!"

23 Sing to the LORD, all the earth!
   Tell of his salvation from day to day.
24 Declare his glory among the nations,
   his marvelous works among all the peoples!
25 For great is the LORD, and greatly to be praised,
   and he is to be feared above all gods.
26 For all the gods of the peoples are worthless idols,
   but the LORD made the heavens.
27 Splendor and majesty are before him;
   strength and joy are in his place.

28 Ascribe to the LORD, O families of the peoples,
   ascribe to the LORD glory and strength!
29 Ascribe to the LORD the glory due his name;
   bring an offering and come before him!
   Worship the LORD in the splendor of holiness;[1]
30 tremble before him, all the earth;
   yes, the world is established; it shall never be moved.
31 Let the heavens be glad, and let the earth rejoice,
   and let them say among the nations, "The LORD reigns!"
32 Let the sea roar, and all that fills it;
   let the field exult, and everything in it!
33 Then shall the trees of the forest sing for joy
   before the LORD, for he comes to judge the earth.
34 Oh give thanks to the LORD, for he is good;
   for his steadfast love endures forever!

35 Say also:

"Save us, O God of our salvation,
   and gather and deliver us from among the nations,
that we may give thanks to your holy name
   and glory in your praise.

[1] Or in holy attire

400

36 Blessed be
   from e
Then all the people said

Worship Before the Ark
37 So David left Asap
LORD to minister regul
and his[1] sixty-eight br
were to be gatekeeper
before the tabernacle
burnt offerings to the
evening, to do all tha
41 With them were H
named to give thank
and Jeduthun had tr
song. The sons of Jed
43 Then all the pe
his household.

The LORD's Covena
17 Now when D
   hold, I dwell
under a tent." 2 An
with you."

3 But that same
servant David, 'Th
in. 5 For I have not
I have gone from
I have moved wi
whom I comman
a house of cedar?
says the LORD of
prince over my p
have cut off all y
the name of the
Israel and will p
no more. And v
that I appointe
Moreover, I de
are fulfilled in
of your own sc
and I will esta
me a son. I wi
before you, 14
his throne sh
in accordance

David's Pray
16 Then K
God, and w
small thing
great while

[1] Hebrew their 2 T

Creating Letter Stickers

1 CHRONICLES 16:31–34

I love Christmas. It's my favorite holiday! As I was putting up our Christmas tree, the idea came to me to create a journal page with a Christmas tree motif. Now I know the tradition of Christmas trees came much later than the Bible, but it's such a big part of my family's celebration that I wanted to include it in my Bible.

I searched the word *tree* in the Bible app YouVersion and read through the verses I found until I came across one that I wanted to investigate further. The verses I found for this page are part of David's song of thanks when dedicating the tabernacle. In this section, David describes how all of creation will praise the Lord with intense joy when the Messiah, Christ, comes. (When using an app to search for a particular term, be sure to read the surrounding verses or whole chapter so you don't take the verse out of context.)

Although I love to do my own hand lettering, I'm not always able to give it a nice smooth look because I take medication that can make my hands shaky. During those times I either just sketch out the words in pencil, then ink over them at a later time or I head to my computer to create my own letter stickers using clear labels made for addressing packages.

A Fount of Fonts

As you probably know, the Internet is filled with tons of terrific fonts and searching for the perfect one to use can be really fun. Some of my favorite places to find fonts online are dafont.com and myfonts.com, which have a lot of free ones. I purchase many of the fonts I use from creativemarket.com as well because I can buy a license to use them in any projects I sell.

SUPPLIES

Font: *Hello Script Regular*

Computer

Inkjet or laser printer

Printer paper

Scissors

Temporary adhesive: *Glue Dots*

Clear printable sticker sheet: *Avery 18665* (make sure it's compatible with your computer)

Die-cutting machine (optional)

Green and black patterned papers: *Lawn Fawn* 6" x 6" (15 x 15 cm) paper pad in "Peace Joy Love"; *Echo Park* 6" x 6" paper pad in "Christmas Cheer"

Ruler

Triangle, rectangle, and star templates on page 147 (optional)

Glue stick

Yellow card stock

Pencil

Eraser

Paper trimmer (optional)

Craft knife and craft mat (optional)

Bracket sticker (included at back of book)

TECHNIQUES

Creating letter stickers

Paper crafting

TIP
The word art is provided on page 153 if you'd like to scan it instead of designing your own.

1 Choose a font you want to use (I used Hello Script Regular) and install it onto your computer. In a word-processing or photo-editing program, type out your text. Make sure it will fit the space on your page. You may want some words to be larger or smaller than others. On a sheet of plain printer paper, print out the words.

2 Cut out the words, leaving some in groups as I did. Cut as close to the words as you can, being careful not to cut into the letters.

3 Place temporary adhesive on the back of the words. Arrange the words on your page, noticing if you need to resize any of the words. Make any corrections you need to before printing on the actual sticker paper.

4 Load the clear sticker paper into your printer and print out the text.

5 Use scissors or a digital die-cutting machine to cut out the words. Remove the temporary words and adhere the sticker words to your page.

TIP
Using 6" x 6" (15 x 15 cm) paper pads for these types of projects is convenient, the print is usually scaled to a smaller size, and you get a variety of designs.

6 Choose a few green papers and one black one. Hand cut or use a die-cutting machine to cut out nine triangles roughly 1½" (3.8 cm) wide at the base and about 2" (5 cm) tall out of the green papers and three ½" x 3" (1.3 x 7.5 cm) rectangles for the tree trunks out of the black paper. (You can also trace the triangle and rectangle templates on page 147.)

7 Decide which triangles to layer together for each tree and glue them together with a glue stick. Glue the rectangle tree trunks onto the trees.

8 Adhere the trees to the page with the glue stick. If placing a tree so it goes off the edge of the page, use scissors or a trimmer to trim the area.

9 On yellow card stock use a pencil to draw three stars (or use the templates on page 147). Use scissors, a die-cutting machine, or a craft knife on a craft mat to cut them out. Adhere them to the page with the glue stick, then trim off any excess. Add the bracket sticker to highlight the verse.

works of the flesh are evident: sexual immorality, impurity, sensuality, [20] idolatry, sorcery, enmity, strife, jealousy, fits of anger, rivalries, dissensions, divisions, [21] envy, drunkenness, orgies, and things like these. I warn you, as I warned you before, that those who do such things will not inherit the kingdom of God. [22] But the fruit of the Spirit is love, joy, peace, patience, kindness, goodness, faithfulness, [23] gentleness, self-control; against such things there is no law. [24] And those who belong to Christ Jesus have crucified the flesh with its passions and desires. [25] If we live by the Spirit, let us also keep in step with the Spirit. [26] Let us not become conceited, provoking one another, envying one another.

Bear One Another's Burdens

6 Brothers,[2] if anyone is caught in any transgression, you who are spiritual should restore him in a spirit of gentleness. Keep watch on yourself, lest you too be tempted. [2] Bear one another's burdens, and so fulfill the law of Christ. [3] For if anyone thinks he is something, when he is nothing, he deceives himself. [4] But let each one test his own work, and then his reason to boast will be in himself alone and not in his neighbor. [5] For each will have to bear his own load.

[6] Let the one who is taught the word share all good things with the one who teaches. [7] Do not be deceived: God is not mocked, for whatever one sows, that will he also reap. [8] For the one who sows to his own flesh will from the flesh reap corruption, but the one who sows to the Spirit will from the Spirit reap eternal life. [9] And let us not grow weary of doing good, for in due season we will reap, if we do not give up. [10] So then, as we have opportunity, let us do good to everyone, and especially to those who are of the household of faith.

Final Warning and Benediction

[11] See with what large letters I am writing to you with my own hand. [12] It is those who want to make a good showing in the flesh who would force you to be circumcised, and only in order that they may not be persecuted for the cross of Christ. [13] For even those who are circumcised do not themselves keep the law, but they desire to have you circumcised that they may boast in your flesh. [14] But far be it from me to boast except in the cross of our Lord Jesus Christ, by which[3] the world has been crucified to me, and I to the world. [15] For neither circumcision counts for anything, nor uncircumcision, but a new creation. [16] And as for all who walk by this rule, peace and mercy be upon them, and upon the Israel of God.

[17] From now on let no one cause me trouble, for I bear on my body the marks of Jesus.

[18] The grace of our Lord Jesus Christ be with your spirit, brothers. Amen.

LOVE
JOY
PEACE
PATIENCE
KINDNESS
GOODNESS
FAITHFULNESS
GENTLENESS
SELF-CONTROL

[1] Some manuscripts add murder [2] Or Brothers and sisters; also verse 18 [3] Or through whom

Traceable Word Art

GALATIANS 5:22–23

The Fruit of the Spirit is a list of traits that demonstrate that Jesus has come into his followers' lives and made His home in their hearts. When we accept Jesus as our personal Lord and Savior, the Holy Spirit plants the seeds of these fruits into our lives, and it is with His help that we can grow and mature in our journey with the Lord.

These traits might not come naturally for everyone, but with the Holy Spirit's help you will mature and glorify God. I like to read through this list periodically and check in with the Lord to see where I can ask Him to help me grow.

While rereading this list one day, I felt the Lord nudging me to create a page about it. I knew I wanted to list the attributes as a strong visual reminder. I designed the wording on my computer, then traced it. This is an easy way to incorporate lettering into your journal, even if hand lettering isn't your forte.

Fruit was the obvious choice to illustrate this list. If pineapple is not your favorite (as it is mine), try another or even multiple fruits. Choose a fruit that is delicious to you and that will remind you when you eat it to reflect on the "Fruit of the Spirit."

SUPPLIES

Pencil

Eraser

Pineapple drawing (page 151; optional)

Computer

Font: *Kraft Nine Regular*

Printer

Printer paper

Paper trimmer or scissors

Light box or tablet device with light box app

Washi tape

Colored pencils: *Prismacolor Premier* in process red, crimson red, orange, canary yellow, spring green, aquamarine, ultramarine, violet, lime peel, olive green, and light umber

Black pen: *Faber-Castell PITT Artist Pen* (small nib)

TECHNIQUES

Creating word art

Tracing

Drawing

Colored pencils

Tracing Tips

Because Bible pages are so thin, it's easy to trace art and lettering through them. There are a couple ways to do it. The most common method is to use a light box, or light pad. There are a number of small, thinner light boxes available that work well for tracing onto Bible pages. Follow Steps 3–5 on pages 76 and 77 for step-by-step instructions.

If you have a tablet device, you can download an app that works as a light box. Many of them are free. Use it the same way as a light box, but take care not to damage your screen.

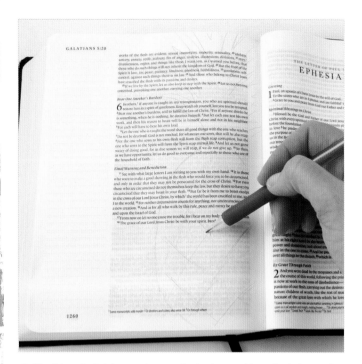

1 Start by sketching out your fruit shape. Most fruit is made up of simple shapes. For this pineapple, I created a large oval and added a spiky crown. For the texture on it I made X marks. The image is provided on page 151 if you prefer to trace it.

2 On your computer with a word-processing program, create a new document with the same page size as your Bible. Find a font you like (I used *Kraft Nine Regular*; see page 71 for resources for free fonts), type out the list of characteristics, then print it out. Trim off any extra blank space from the paper.

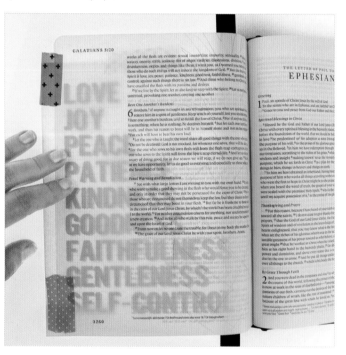

3 Place the light box underneath the Bible page. Depending on the size of your light box you may need to support it with books to keep the surface level. Place your printed paper on the light box underneath your Bible page and position it where you want the text to go.

4 Tape down the corners of the printed paper and the Bible page with washi tape to hold them in place.

5 Trace the letters with a pencil.

6 Randomly color in the letters with a variety of colored pencils. You can leave the page on the light box while you color or remove it.

TIP
Creating this page has inspired me to create a similar piece I can place on my wall. See page 31 for ideas on how to expand your faith journaling outside of your Bible.

7 Color in the fruit with colored pencils. I used canary yellow and orange with light umber Xs for the pineapple and spring green and olive green for the spiky crown.

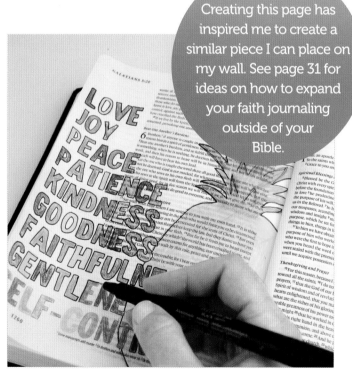

8 Carefully trace around the letters and the fruit with the black pen.

Incorporating Hymns

LUKE 2

The wonderful story of Jesus's birth is told in Luke 2, and it always makes me think of the Christmas song "Joy to the World," even though it wasn't originally written about Christmas but about the Second Coming of Christ. Because this song reminds me of Jesus's birth, which wouldn't be as joyful without His resurrection and promise to come again, I wanted to include a copy of it in my Bible. Adding it as a tip-in is a nice way to celebrate Christmas and this wonderful melody inspired by Psalm 98.

I considered just incorporating the sheet music into my Bible page, but I wanted to highlight it with artwork that reminded me of Christmas. That season has a lot of different motifs to choose from, and I chose to use holly, which represents the crown of thorns Jesus wore when He was crucified, and holly berries, which represent the drops of blood the thorns produced. For this page, I used watercolor pencils, which are activated with water after coloring. They are a wonderful medium for journaling because you have a little more control with them than when working with watercolor paints.

SUPPLIES

Pencil

Eraser

Watercolor pencils: *Faber-Castell Aquarelles* in pale geranium lake, permanent carmine, grass green, and earth green yellowish

Water brush

Paper towels

Acrylic block or craft mat

Markers: *Faber-Castell PITT Artist Pens* in May green, permanent green olive, chromium green opaque, and black (small nib)

Colored pencils: *Prismacolor Premier* in crimson red, light umber, and olive green

Adhesive: *Scotch Advanced Tape Glider (ATG)*

Sheet music

Patterned paper: Echo Park *"Season's Greetings"*

Scissors

Paper trimmer (optional)

Washi tape

Tab (from die-cut sheet at back of book)

"Christmas" sticker: *The Girls' Paperie*

TECHNIQUES

Watercolor pencils

Drawing

Adding tip-ins

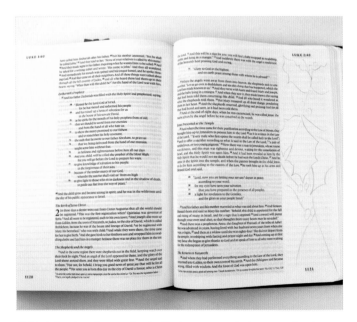

1 Lightly sketch out the holly, leaves, and pine needles in the margin of the page as shown here. Don't worry about making them perfect.

the Lord. [12]And this will be a sign for you: you will find a baby wrapped in swaddling cloths and lying in a manger." [13] And suddenly there was with the angel a multitude of the heavenly host praising God and saying,

[14] "Glory to God in the highest,
    and on earth peace among those with whom he is pleased!"[1]

[15]When the angels went away f

2 Use watercolor pencils to quickly color in the leaves and stem. You don't need to fill in the image perfectly as you might do with traditional colored pencils.

3 Use a water brush to paint each color separately. To avoid mixing colors, be sure to allow one color to dry and to rinse off and dry your brush on a paper towel before moving on to another color.

Tips for Working with Watercolor Pencils

Using watercolor pencils is a great way to combine drawing with painting and get a professional look.

- When using watercolor pencils, make sure they are well sharpened and color with the side of the pencil over larger spaces and the tip of the pencil in tiny ones.

- It's best to start with light pressure, as you can always add more color. Use a slightly harder pressure over areas you want to be shaded darker.

- Your illustration doesn't need to be filled in completely or perfectly, because once you activate it with water it will all smooth out.

- If you don't have the perfect color in your collection, you can color your design with multiple colors that, when combined, become that perfect color.

- Watercolor pencils (and watercolors in general) react differently on different types of surfaces. On the super-thin pages of a Bible, you most likely will have some wrinkling, and if you overwork the paper with your paintbrush, it may tear. So with that in mind, err on the side of using less water and gentle pressure.

- I like to let my watercolored pages air-dry rather than use a heat gun to speed my page along beacuse it tends to change the texture of the page from a soft bendable paper into a stiffer, crunchy one.

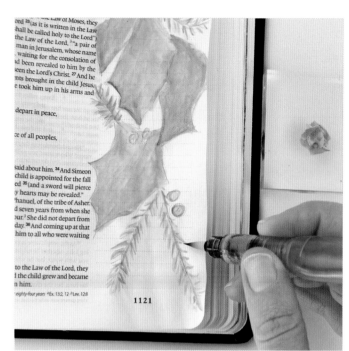

4 Color in the holly berries with a watercolor pencil, then paint them with the water brush.

5 On an acrylic block or craft mat, scribble a bit of the green shades of the markers. Use your water brush to pick up some of the green and then paint the pine needles with quick, short strokes. Using a variety of shades of green will make it look like they are individual needles.

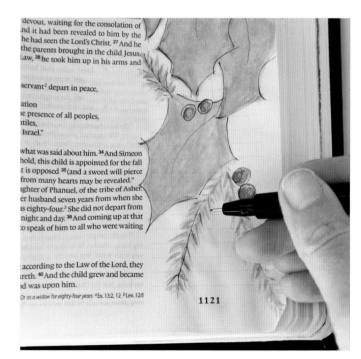

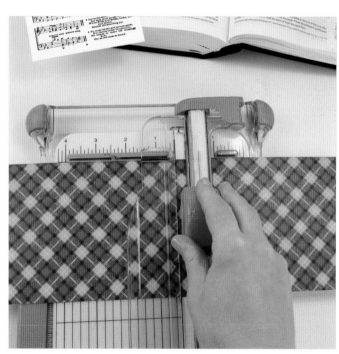

6 Once the page is painted and dry, use a colored pencil to outline the holly berries, add a touch of brown color to the stems, and add a different shade and texture to the pine needles. Use a fine-tip black pen to add sketchy lines.

7 Cut a piece of patterned paper about 1½" (3.8 cm) larger than the sheet music.

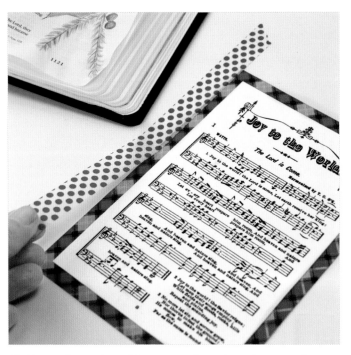

8 Use adhesive to mount the sheet music onto the center of the patterned paper.

9 Use a piece of washi tape to adhere it to the page: Lay the washi tape along the left edge of the tip-in, leaving half of the width of the tape hanging off.

10 Create a lengthwise crease in the washi tape by folding it in half.

11 Adhere the other half of the tape to the Bible.

Sheet Music Ephemera

Many modern churches no longer sing old-fashioned hymns, which is really a shame. They are composed with such rich music and written with a poetry we just don't hear in a lot of modern Christian music. Because they contain so many Bible truths and doctrines, they are perfect for incorporating into your Bible art journal. The benefit of many churches getting rid of hymnals, though, is that they are easy to find and reasonably priced to add to your art journaling supplies. Pick up a copy at a used book or thrift store, or buy one from a reputable online seller. Read through the eloquent poetry of these songs and look for ways to incorporate them into your art. Use just a line out of one or a hymn in its entirety. An old hymnal or sheet music that you want to use for this project is perfect, but if you don't have one, you can search online for public domain sheet music and save it to your computer. Resize it, if needed, and print it onto card stock.

12 To create a bookmark, punch out the red die-cut tab found at the back of the book. Adhere the "Christmas" sticker to it, and attach it to the page with a piece of washi tape.

55 There were also many women there, looking on from a distance, who had followed Jesus from Galilee, ministering to him, 56 among whom were Mary Magdalene and Mary the mother of James and Joseph and the mother of the sons of Zebedee.

Jesus Is Buried

57 a When it was evening, there came a rich man from Arimathea, named Joseph, who also was a disciple of Jesus. 58 He went to Pilate and asked for the body of Jesus. Then Pilate ordered it to be given to him. 59 And Joseph took the body and wrapped it in a clean linen shroud 60 and laid it in his own new tomb, which he had cut in the rock. And he rolled a great stone to the entrance of the tomb and went away. 61 Mary Magdalene and the other Mary were there, sitting opposite the tomb.

The Guard at the Tomb

62 The next day, that is, after the day of Preparation, the chief priests and the Pharisees gathered before Pilate 63 and said, "Sir, we remember how that impostor said, while he was still alive, 'After three days I will rise.' 64 Therefore order the tomb to be made secure until the third day, lest his disciples go and steal him away and tell the people, 'He has risen from the dead,' and the last fraud will be worse than the first." 65 Pilate said to them, "You have a guard [1] of soldiers. Go, make it as secure as you can." 66 So they went and made the tomb secure by sealing the stone and setting a guard.

The Resurrection

28 b Now after the Sabbath, toward the dawn of the first day of the week, Mary Magdalene and the other Mary went to see the tomb. 2 And behold, there was a great earthquake, for an angel of the Lord descended from heaven and came and rolled back the stone and sat on it. 3 His appearance was like lightning, and his clothing white as snow. 4 And for fear of him the guards trembled and became like dead men. 5 But the angel said to the women, "Do not be afraid, for I know that you seek Jesus who was crucified. 6 He is not here, for he has risen, as he said. Come, see the place where he [2] lay. 7 Then go quickly and tell his disciples that he has risen from the dead, and behold, he is going before you to Galilee; there you will see him. See, I have told you." 8 So they departed quickly from the tomb with fear and great joy, and ran to tell his disciples. 9 And behold, Jesus met them and said, "Greetings!" And they came up and took hold of his feet and worshiped him. 10 Then Jesus said to them, "Do not be afraid; go and tell my brothers to go to Galilee, and there they will see me."

Report of the Guard

11 While they were going, behold, some of the guard went into the city and told the chief priests all that had taken place. 12 And when they had assembled with the elders and taken counsel, they gave a sufficient sum of money to the soldiers 13 and said, "Tell people, 'His disciples came by night and stole him away while we were asleep.' 14 And if this comes to the governor's ears, we will satisfy him and keep you out of trouble." 15 So they took the money and did as they were directed. And this story has been spread among the Jews to this day.

The Great Commission

16 Now the eleven disciples went to Galilee, to the mountain to which Jesus had directed them. 17 And when they saw him they worshiped him, but some doubted. 18 And Jesus came and said to them, "All authority in heaven and on earth has been given to me. 19 Go therefore and make disciples of all nations, baptizing them in [3] the name of the Father and of the Son and of the Holy Spirit, 20 teaching them to observe all that I have commanded you. And behold, I am with you always, to the end of the age."

1 Or Take a guard 2 Some manuscripts the Lord 3 Or into a For 27:57-61 see parallels Mark 15:42-47; Luke 23:50-56; John 19:38-42 b For 28:1-8 see parallels Mark 16:1-8; Luke 24:1-10; John 20:1

Crayons: Two Ways

MATTHEW 28:16–20

At the end of Matthew 28, Jesus commands all of His followers to participate in the process of helping others become disciples of the Lord. This is called the Great Commission. Our church recently had a preaching series in which we were taught how to work together to share God's love with those the Holy Spirit was drawing into our lives.

I thought of the symbols I could use to illustrate this idea. I wrote out the verse by hand, underlined all the key words in it, and then circled the ones that I thought would make good word pictures, such as "go" and "all nations." I like to use an arrow for action words like "go." "All nations" made me think of the Earth, and then when I thought about the love we are commanded to share with all the people in the world, I decided on a heart.

The techniques I used on this page involve two types of crayons—water-soluble ones and the "regular" ones most people are more familiar with—used in two ways: First, I used regular crayons under the water-soluble ones to act as a resist, then I colored with the regular crayons over the water-soluble ones to variegate the color and give it some texture.

SUPPLIES

Heart map design (page 153; optional)

Pencil

Eraser

Light box or tablet device with light box app (optional)

Water-soluble crayons: *Reeves Water Soluble Wax Pastels*

Water brush

Crayons: *Faber-Castell Paper Crafter Crayons* (red/yellow and blue/green sets)

Crayon sharpener: *Faber-Castell Trio Sharpening Box Colour Grip*

Scratch paper

Pens: *Staedtliner Triplus Fineliner* in blue; *Faber-Castell PITT Artist Pen* in black (small nib)

TECHNIQUES

Drawing or tracing

Water-soluble crayons

"Regular" crayons

Creating a resist

Lettering

1 Using a pencil, sketch out the heart map design or trace the one on page 153 by placing the design on a light box and placing the Bible page on top of it. Leave off the word art inside the design for now.

2 Color in the heart map using various shades of water-soluble crayons and allow it to dry.

3 Activate the crayons with a water brush, being careful to decide when you want colors to mix and when you don't. Allow to dry.

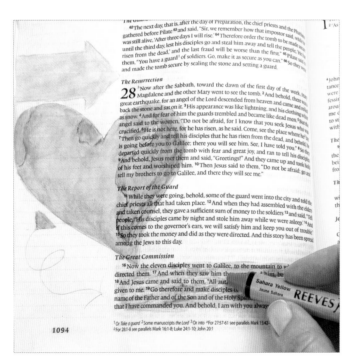

4 Color the large arrow with a blue water-soluble crayon and the smaller arrow with an orange one. Color over the Bible verses with two or three colors of water-soluble crayons and activate them with the water brush.

5 With Paper Crafter Crayons, color lightly over the colors in the heart to give them texture. Mix colors so hints of water-soluble crayon color peek through. For example, if the water-soluble crayon was light blue, color over it lightly with a darker blue and purple regular crayons. Over the pink water-soluble crayon, color with orange or red.

6 Using a white Paper Crafter's Crayon that has been sharpened to a point, draw stars around the heart and arrows.

7 On scratch paper, scribble the black water-soluble crayon, use a water brush to pick up some color, then paint around the art. To gradually fade the color, add more water from the brush. The white stars should show through.

8 Write in the words "Go therefore & make disciples of all nations" with pencil or trace the word art from page 153 if you prefer.

9 Using a fine-tip blue pen, outline the large arrow with a solid line and then a dashed line and then trace over the words. There are also two small arrows inside the heart to trace over.

10 Using a fine-tip black pen, double outline the heart and the "continents" inside the heart. Continue using the black pen to trace the words in the heart. Trace the curly arrow with the black pen. Erase any pencil marks on the page. Add additional stars with a white pen.

Journaling over the Page

1 CHRONICLES 16:8–13

When I'm studying God's Word and worshiping Him in Bible art journaling, I usually don't like to obscure scripture words with my artwork. But I know that others may not have the same convictions, so I wanted to create a page where I did cover some of the text in order to emphasize the portion that God had drawn me to.

1 Chronicles 16 takes place after the Ark of the covenant, the ancient symbol of the Lord's presence, was first brought to Jerusalem. It was a time of celebration with food, music, and dancing. As I read over David's song of thanks to the Lord in this chapter, I saw a certain key word used repeatedly: "seek." In the ESV version of the Bible it's used in verses 10 and 11, saying that those who seek the Lord should be rejoicing and "seeking the Lord, and His strength, and His presence continually!" That really spoke to me because at the time I needed that reminder. Despite all the obstacles of life, Believers can rejoice because He is good all of the time and gives us the strength we need. We can trust that what He is allowing to happen in our lives is being used to bring us into His presence.

SUPPLIES

Sponge brush

Clear gesso: *Prima Marketing Inc.*

Black pens: *Faber-Castell PITT Artist Pens* (fine and medium nibs)

Sticky notes

Acrylic paint: *DecoArt Americana* in sea aqua and desert turquoise

Palette paper

Acrylic glazing liquid: *Golden*

Scraper

"Seek" sticker (provided at back of book)

Cotton swabs

White letter stickers: *Studio Calico*

Ruler

White gel pen: *Signo*

TECHNIQUES

Acrylic paint

Masking

Altering letter stickers

1 With a sponge brush, apply a thin coat of clear gesso over the entire page to prime it, so that the paint will not bleed through the page. Allow it to dry and then do the same thing for the back of the page so that anything done on that side in the future won't bleed through to this page.

singers who should play loudly on musical instruments, on harps and lyres and cymbals, to raise sounds of joy. [17] So the Levites appointed Heman the son of Joel; and of his brothers Asaph the son of Berechiah, and of the sons of Merari, their brothers, Ethan the son of Kushaiah; [18] and with them their brothers of the second order, Zechariah, Jaaziel, Shemiramoth, Jehiel, Unni, Eliab, Benaiah, Maaseiah, Mattithiah, Eliphelehu, and Mikneiah, and the gatekeepers Obed-edom and Jeiel. [19] The singers, Heman, Asaph, and Ethan, were to sound bronze cymbals; [20] Zechariah, Aziel, Shemiramoth, Jehiel, Unni, Eliab, Maaseiah, and Benaiah were to play harps according to Alamoth; [21] but Mattithiah, Eliphelehu, Mikneiah, Obed-edom, Jeiel, and Azaziah were to lead with harps according to the Sheminith. [22] Chenaniah, leader of the Levites in music, should direct the music, for he understood it. [23] Berechiah and Elkanah were to be gatekeepers for the ark. [24] Shebaniah, Joshaphat, Nethanel, Amasai, Zechariah, Benaiah, and Eliezer, the priests, should blow the trumpets before the ark of God. Obed-edom and Jehiah were to be gatekeepers for the ark.

[25] So David and the elders of Israel and the commanders of thousands went to bring up the ark of the covenant of the LORD from the house of Obed-edom with rejoicing. [26] And because God helped the Levites who were carrying the ark of the covenant of the LORD, they sacrificed seven bulls and seven rams. [27] David was clothed with a robe of fine linen, as also were all the Levites who were carrying the ark, and Chenaniah the leader of the music of the singers. And David wore a linen ephod. [28] So all Israel brought up the ark of the covenant of the LORD with shouting, to the sound of the horn, trumpets, and cymbals, and made loud music on harps and lyres.

[29] And as the ark of the covenant of the LORD came to the city of David, Michal the daughter of Saul looked out of the window and saw King David dancing and celebrating, and she despised him in her heart.

The Ark Placed in a Tent

And they brought in the ark of God and set it inside the tent that David had pitched for it, and they offered burnt offerings and peace offerings before God. [2] And when David had finished offering the burnt offerings and the peace offerings, he blessed the people in the name of the LORD [3] and distributed to all Israel, both men and women, to each a loaf of bread, a portion of meat, and a cake of raisins.

[4] Then he appointed some of the Levites as ministers before the ark of the LORD, to invoke, to thank, and to praise the LORD, the God of Israel. [5] Asaph was the chief, and second to him were Zechariah, Jeiel, Shemiramoth, Jehiel, Mattithiah, Eliab, Benaiah, Obed-edom, and Jeiel, who were to play harps and lyres; Asaph was to sound the cymbals, [6] and Benaiah and Jahaziel the priests were to blow trumpets regularly before the ark of the covenant of God. [7] Then on that day David first appointed that thanksgiving be sung to the LORD by Asaph and his brothers.

David's Song of Thanks

[8] Oh give thanks to the LORD; call upon his name;
    make known his deeds among the peoples!
[9] Sing to him, sing praises to him;
    tell of all his wondrous works!
[10] Glory in his holy name;
    let the hearts of those who seek the LORD rejoice!
[11] Seek the LORD and his strength;
    seek his presence continually!
[12] Remember the wondrous works that he has done,
    his miracles and the judgments he uttered,
[13] O offspring of Israel his servant,
    children of Jacob, his chosen ones!

[1] Compare Septuagint, Syriac, Vulgate; the meaning of the Hebrew is uncertain

seek the Lord His Strength His Presence

2 Using a fine-tip black pen, outline the verses with a rectangle. Just freehand draw it multiple times around the verses, not worrying if the lines are perfectly straight. As you overlap the lines it becomes a design instead of just a rectangle.

3 Place sticky notes over the verse and outline to keep that section from getting painted.

4 Squirt a small amount of turquoise and aqua acrylic paint onto the palette paper. Add a small amount of acrylic glazing liquid to each of the paints and mix the paint and glaze together with the scraper to give the paint a bit more transparency once it dries.

5 Remove the "seek" sticker from the back of the book and place it on the page as a mask.

6 With the scraper, pick up a small amount of one color of paint. Scrape the paint onto the page. Take some of the other color of paint and scrape it over the page and mask, too. The colors can overlap or not depending on the look you want. Keep alternating colors until you get as much of the page covered as you like. Let the paint dry.

7 Carefully remove the "seek" mask.

8 If some paint seeped under the mask, you can clean it up with a damp cotton swab; just be careful not to overwork it or the page could tear.

9 Remove the sticky notes and repeat Step 6 to fill in the area to the right of the scripture.

10 With a medium-tip black pen, carefully outline the word "seek" to make it stand out.

11 Working with the white letter stickers still stuck onto the product packaging, use a fine-tip black pen to doodle different patterns onto each letter for each word you are spelling (Lord, Strength, Presence).

12 To apply the letter stickers to the page and make sure they are straight, place just the bottom edge of each sticker onto a ruler.

13 Once the word or phrase is complete, place the ruler on the page where the word should go and press on the letters as you remove the ruler.

14 Use the white gel pen to add "the," ""His," and "His" on the page, too.

15 Outline all of the letters and words with a fine-tip black pen.

If you want the scripture on the page to be more visible, try dipping a sponge dabber into the paint and pouncing it onto the page to give a softer look.

WHEN
you
ADD
your
NOT
enough
to
Christ's
MORE
than
enough
miracles
HAPPEN

the towns. 14 When he went ashore he saw a great crowd, and he had compassion on them and healed their sick. 15 Now when it was evening, the disciples came to him and said, "This is a desolate place, and the day is now over; send the crowds away to go into the villages and buy food for themselves." 16 But Jesus said, "They need not go away; you give them something to eat." 17 They said to him, "We have only five loaves here and two fish." 18 And he said, "Bring them here to me." 19 Then he ordered the crowds to sit down on the grass, and taking the five loaves and the two fish, he looked up to heaven and said a blessing. Then he broke the loaves and gave them to the disciples, and the disciples gave them to the crowds. 20 And they all ate and were satisfied. And they took up twelve baskets full of the broken pieces left over. 21 And those who ate were about five thousand men, besides women and children.

Jesus Walks on the Water

22 a Immediately he made the disciples get into the boat and go before him to the other side, while he dismissed the crowds. 23 And after he had dismissed the crowds, he went up on the mountain by himself to pray. When evening came, he was there alone, 24 but the boat by this time was a long way[1] from the land,[2] beaten by the waves, for the wind was against them. 25 And in the fourth watch of the night he came to them, walking on the sea. 26 But when the disciples saw him walking on the sea, they were terrified, and said, "It is a ghost!" and they cried out in fear. 27 But immediately Jesus spoke to them, saying, "Take heart; it is I. Do not be afraid." 28 And Peter answered him, "Lord, if it is you, command me to come to you on the water." 29 He said, "Come." So Peter got out of the boat and walked on the water and came to Jesus. 30 But when he saw the wind,[3] he was afraid, and beginning to sink he cried out, "Lord, save me." 31 Jesus immediately reached out his hand and took hold of him, saying to him, "O you of little faith, why did you doubt?" 32 And when they got into the boat, the wind ceased. 33 And those in the boat worshiped him, saying, "Truly you are the Son of God."

Jesus Heals the Sick in Gennesaret

34 b And when they had crossed over, they came to land at Gennesaret. 35 And when the men of that place recognized him, they sent around to all that region and brought to him all who were sick 36 and implored him that they might only touch the fringe of his garment. And as many as touched it were made well.

Traditions and Commandments

15 Then Pharisees and scribes came to Jesus from Jerusalem and said, 2 "Why do your disciples break the tradition of the elders? For they do not wash their hands when they eat." 3 He answered them, "And why do you break the commandment of God for the sake of your tradition? 4 For God commanded, 'Honor your father and your mother,' and, 'Whoever reviles father or mother must surely die.' 5 But you say, 'If anyone tells his father or his mother, "What you would have gained from me is given to God," 6 he need not honor his father.' So for the sake of your tradition you have made void the word[5] of God. 7 You hypocrites! Well did Isaiah prophesy of you, when he said:

8 "'This people honors me with their lips,
but their heart is far from me;
9 in vain do they worship me,
teaching as doctrines the commandments of men.'"

1 Greek *many stadia*, a *stadion* was about 607 feet or 185 meters 2 Some manuscripts *was out on the sea* 3 Some manuscripts *strong wind* 4 Or *is an offering* 5 Some manuscripts *law* a For 14:22-33 see parallels Mark 6:45-52; John 6:16-21 b For 14:34-36 see parallel Mark 6:53-56 c For 15:1-20 see parallel Mark 7:1-23 d Ex. 20:12 e Ex. 21:17 f Isa. 29:13

What Defiles a Person

10 And he called the peo[ple]
not what goes into the mo[uth]
this defiles a person. 12 T[hen]
the Pharisees were offen[ded]
[p]lant that my heavenly [Father]
they are blind guides.[a] A[nd]
Peter said to him, "Expla[in]
understanding? 17 Do yo[u not]
stomach and is expelled[?]
and this defiles a perso[n]
sexual immorality, the[ft]
to eat with unwashed [hands]

The Faith of a Canaa[nite Woman]

21 b And Jesus went
22 And behold, a Can[aanite]
mercy on me, O Lor[d]
23 But he did not ans[wer]
"Send her away, for [she]
lost sheep of the ho[use]
help me." 26 And he [answered]
it to the dogs." 27 S[he said]
their masters' tabl[e]
done for you as yo[u desire]

Jesus Heals Man[y]

29 Jesus went
up on the moun[tain]
with them the [lame]
put them at his [feet]
saw the mute s[peak]
And they glori[fied]

Jesus Feeds th[e Four Thousand]

32 b Then Je[sus]
because the[y]
unwilling to [send]
said to him, [Where]
a crowd?" 34 [And Jesus]
and a few s[mall fish]
the seven lo[aves]
to the disc[iples]
satisfied. A[nd]
[th]ey were f[our thousand]
the crow[d]

The Pha[risees]

16 A[nd]
[th]e
will b[e]
for t[he]

Stenciling with Watercolors

MATTHEW 14:13–21

I was studying the Bible passages about the miracle of Jesus multiplying a little boy's lunch to feed thousands of people when I came upon the quote, "When you add your not enough to Christ's more than enough, miracles happen," from Sheila Walsh, a Christian musician and inspirational speaker and author. That quote reminds me that even though at times I feel like I'm not enough, God is and He will work in and through me to accomplish things that will glorify Him. God longs to take the humble, seemingly insignificant person and to use her, so, as 1 Corinthians 1:28-29 says, she won't boast about herself but with praise will magnify Him.

This miraculous passage and the quote I used both have some arithmetic in them that I wanted to come across in the artwork. I used the symbol for addition, a plus sign, to illustrate how when Believers bring their limited expectations to Jesus, He uses them for His glory. I wanted to cover the entire page, but still wanted it to be transparent enough to see the scripture, so I stenciled it with watercolor paints, which I don't often use with stencils.

SUPPLIES

Sponge brush

Clear gesso: *Prima Marketing Inc.*

Stencil: *Stencil Girl "Peacock"*

Watercolor paint: *Sakura Koi*

Baby wipes

Stamps: *Illustrated Faith "Elements"* set and *Stampers Anonymous "Mesh"* stamp

Acrylic block

Black ink: *Tsukineko StazOn*

Scratch paper

Plus shape template (page 147)

Card stock

Scissors

Colored pens: *Faber-Castell PITT Artist Pen* in black (small and medium nibs) and geranium lake (brush tip)

Water brush

Pencil

Eraser

Letter and number stickers: *Cosmo Cricket "Just My Type"*

Palette paper, waxed paper, or craft mat

White gel pen: *Signo*

TECHNIQUES

Stenciling

Stamping

Letter stickers

Lettering

1 With a sponge brush, apply a thin coat of clear gesso over the whole page and allow it to dry. The clear gesso prepares the page so the color won't bleed through. It also creates a slicker surface so you can blend the colors together.

2 Place the stencil over the page and then paint over it with the sponge brush and various watercolors.

3 Remove the stencil and allow the page to dry. Use a baby wipe to blend the colors.

Oops, I Already Journaled on That Page!

Once your Bible begins to fill up with all the artwork you've been making, it might get frustrating when you're inspired to create a page on a certain passage, flip open to it, and realize that you've already filled that page for another passage of scripture.

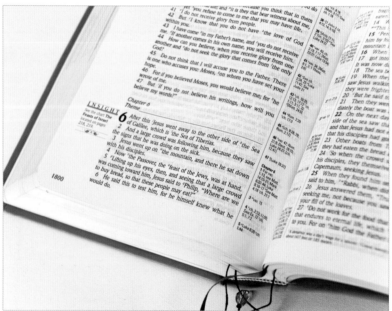

I'm currently studying the book of John, so many of my recent pages have been in that book. For this page I was originally going to use John 6:1–15 as my inspirational verses; however, when I turned there, lo and behold I had already created something on that page for another passage. Remember that many of the stories told in the Gospels (Matthew, Mark, Luke, and John) are repeated within those books, so that we get a multi-person account of what happened. My study Bible, and probably yours as well, has a reference column with cross-references that can lead you to other mentions of that story or lead you to other verses that may help clarify what you've read. So I looked and found that Matthew 14:13–21 tells the same story.

4 Apply the cross stamp to an acrylic block and then ink it up with black ink. Stamp it onto a piece of scratch paper and then quickly stamp it onto your Bible page several times in the lower right and upper right corners. This will give a lighter stamp, so if it covers any of the text you will still be able to read it.

5 Trace the plus shape (see page 147) onto a piece of card stock and cut it out to use as a template. Place the template on your page and draw around it with the pink pen.

6 Use a water brush to blend out the color. Continue to move the plus template around the page, repeating this process. Blend each plus sign as you trace it so the ink won't dry before you have a chance to blend it out.

7 With pencil, write out the words "When you add your not enough to Christ's more than enough miracles happen," applying letter stickers for the words "add" and "more."

8 Trace over the pencil lines with a black pen. Add a shadow to the cross by drawing lines parallel to the left side of the cross and fill it with lines.

9 Place the "add" letter stickers onto a piece of palette paper (or waxed paper or craft mat). Use the pink pen to color the mesh stamp.

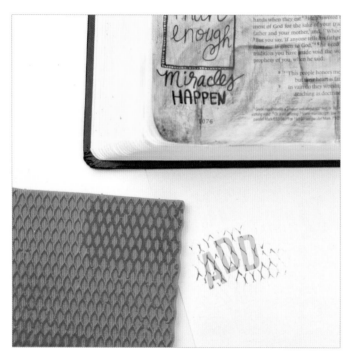

10 Stamp the letter stickers.

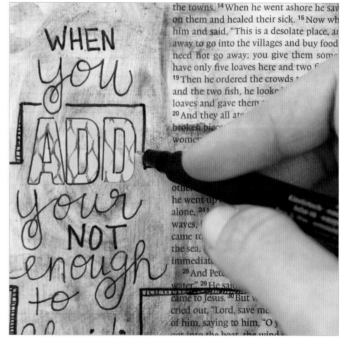

11 Adhere "add" to your Bible margin and then use a fine-tip black pen to trace around all of the letter stickers.

12 Use a white pen to draw stripes on the letters of the "more" stickers.

13 Add sketch marks around the outside of the cross with the white pen.

14 Apply small letter stickers over the reference at the top of the page to spell out "Matthew 14:13." Write a hyphen with the small-tipped black pen and then adhere the "21" stickers.

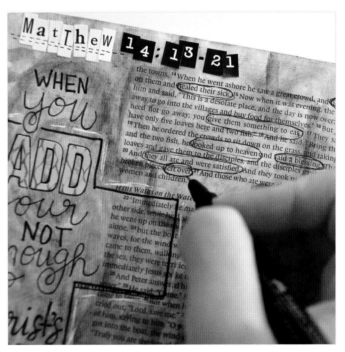

15 Use the small-tipped black pen to circle key words in the scripture passage.

THE FIRST LETTER OF PETER

1 PETER

Greeting

1 Peter, an apostle of Jesus Christ,

To those who are elect exiles of the Dispersion in Pontus, Galatia, Cappadocia, Asia, and Bithynia, ² according to the foreknowledge of God the Father, in the sanctification of the Spirit, for obedience to Jesus Christ and for sprinkling with his blood:

May grace and peace be multiplied to you.

Born Again to a Living Hope

³ Blessed be the God and Father of our Lord Jesus Christ! According to his great mercy, he has caused us to be born again to a living hope through the resurrection of Jesus Christ from the dead, ⁴ to an inheritance that is imperishable, undefiled, and unfading, kept in heaven for you, ⁵ who by God's power are being guarded through faith for a salvation ready to be revealed in the last time. ⁶ In this you rejoice, though now for a little while, if necessary, you have been grieved by various trials, ⁷ so that the tested genuineness of your faith—more precious than gold that perishes though it is tested by fire—may be found to result in praise and glory and honor at the revelation of Jesus Christ. ⁸ Though you have not seen him, you love him. Though you do not now see him, you believe in him and rejoice with joy that is inexpressible and filled with glory, ⁹ obtaining the outcome of your faith, the salvation of your souls.

¹⁰ Concerning this salvation, the prophets who prophesied about the grace that was to be yours searched and inquired carefully, ¹¹ inquiring what person or time the Spirit of Christ in them was indicating when he predicted the sufferings of Christ and the subsequent glories. ¹² It was revealed to them that they were serving not themselves but you, in the things that have now been announced to you through those who preached the good news to you by the Holy Spirit sent from heaven, things into which angels long to look.

Called to Be Holy

¹³ Therefore, preparing your minds for action,¹ and being sober-minded, set your hope fully on the grace that will be brought to you at the revelation of Jesus Christ. ¹⁴ As obedient children, do not be conformed to the passions of your former ignorance, ¹⁵ but as he who called you is holy, you also be holy in all your conduct, ¹⁶ since it is written, ᵃ "You shall be holy, for I am holy." ¹⁷ And if you call on him as Father who judges impartially according to each one's deeds, conduct yourselves with fear throughout the time of your exile, ¹⁸ knowing that you were ransomed from the futile ways inherited from your forefathers, not with perishable things such as silver or gold, ¹⁹ but with the precious blood of Christ, like that of a lamb without blemish or spot. ²⁰ He was foreknown before the foundation of the world but was made manifest in the last times for the sake of you ²¹ who through him are believers in God, who raised him from the dead and gave him glory, so that your faith and hope are in God.

²² Having purified your souls by your obedience to the truth for a sincere brotherly love, love one another earnestly from a pure heart, ²³ since you have been born again, not of perishable seed but of imperishable, through the living and abiding word of God; ²⁴ for

¹ Greek girding up the loins of your mind ᵃLev. 11:44

He is RISEN!

REJOICE

1306

---

²⁵ And this word

A Living Stone

2 So put away newborn salvation— ³

⁴ As you co and precious to be a holy Christ. ⁶ For children, it

So the hono of the

⁷ So the ho

⁸ and

They stu

⁹ But possessi ness int people,

¹¹ Be flesh, a honora deeds

Subm

¹³ B empe and t shou not u every

gen end are this

¹ Gre
ᵇ Isa.

Faux Stained Glass

1 PETER 1:3

Easter, or Resurrection Sunday as many churches call it, is one of Christianity's most important holidays. This is when we celebrate Christ's miraculous resurrection from the dead, and it's because He is alive that we are able to have eternal life (Romans 6:4). That's definitely cause for celebration!

Because Jesus's resurrection has so much significance for me, I wanted to create a page praising Him and this day with these verses from Peter. I used a fun, whimsical stamped cross on this page to represent the joy of Christ's resurrection. The colors are symbolic Easter colors: pink for a fresh beginning, purple for the royalty of the King of Kings, yellow to represent happiness and the rich inheritance we have in Jesus, blue for the start of a new creation, red for Jesus's blood, and orange and green for hope and renewal. Embossing the stamped design in black makes it look like the beautiful stained-glass windows that grace many churches. It also allows a place for the watercolor paint to sit so the colors are less likely to mix.

SUPPLIES

Washi tape

Stamps: *Dare 2B Artzy "Rejoice Tangle"*

Acrylic stamping blocks or *MISTI*

Embossing ink: *Tsukinkeko VersaMark*

Embossing powder: *WOW!* primary ebony regular

Scratch paper

Craft heat gun

Watercolors: *Artist's Loft*

Spray bottle and water

Water brush

Black pen: *Faber-Castell PITT Artist Pen* (extra-small or small nib)

Pink pen: *Faber-Castell GRIP*

TECHNIQUES

Stamping

Embossing

Watercolor

TIP
Trimming the edge of the page with washi tape makes it less likely to tear—and adds design and color to the page!

1 Rip a piece of washi tape to be the length of the page and place it at the edge of the margin.

2 Place the stamps on acrylic blocks, ink them with clear embossing ink, and stamp the page or use a MISTI to stamp the page. (See page 51 for tips on using a MISTI.)

3 Generously sprinkle black embossing powder onto the stamped images.

4 Tap the excess embossing powder off onto a piece of scratch paper.

5 Turn on a craft heat gun and, from a distance of about 8–10" (20–25 cm) away, aim it at the stamped image. Keep the heat gun moving around over it until the embossing powder melts.

6 After the embossing has cooled, dampen the watercolor paints by spraying them with water.

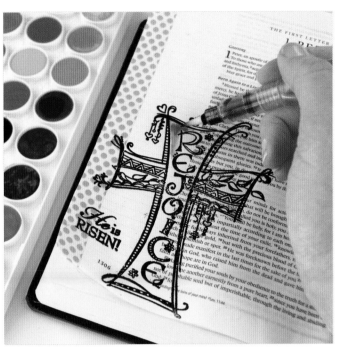

7 Use a water brush to paint in the cross with a variety of watercolors.

8 Apply a wash of watercolor paint to the background of the page and allow it to dry.

9 If after you're finished you notice any embossed areas that need touching up, use a black pen to fill them in. Underline the verse with the pink pen.

Creating Word Art

PSALM 145:10–12

One morning in church, one of the leaders shared how Psalm 145:8–12 speaks of the very theme the pastors were preaching on in the series we were going through—hand-me-downs. You know, those things you want to pass on to the children you have an influence on and to other Believers as well.

When I had a chance to look at the verses myself I just loved how they really did sum up the relationship Believers have with the Lord. He showers compassion on *all* of His creation, and Believers, in thankfulness, praise Him and tell of His glorious kingdom, His power in our lives, and how we've seen Him work in situations and hearts that seemed impossible.

When I'm studying a passage like this that includes God's attributes or ways we should respond, I like to put them in list form. I grab a piece of scratch paper and jot them down, shortening phrases to words I will remember. After I finished a draft of the list, I started hand lettering the words in my Bible margin and embellishing them with complementary images. Don't fret if you hate your handwriting; you can still learn to do hand lettering by practicing, and practicing, and more practicing.

Word Search

Even if you're a commited reader of a particluar version of the Bible, it can be helpful to look at other versions and how they phrase the same piece of scripture. For example, using other Bible versions is often helpful in finding words that will condense the meaning down to fewer words, and they often broaden the meaning of the verses for me. I use the ESV version, but for this passage I really liked how the NLT phrased a lot of the words, so I used some of them in my list.

SUPPLIES

White card stock

Foam brush

Acrylic paint: *Liquitex* in cadmium red deep hue (red) and medium magenta (pink)

Heart punches: *EK Success; Stampin' Up!*

Pencil

Eraser

Hands template (page 151)

Light box or tablet device with light box app (optional)

Circle templates (page 147)

Pens: *Faber-Castell PITT Artist Pens* in black (small nib), cold grey (brush nib), and pale geranium (brush nib)

Ruler (optional)

Glue stick: *Xyron*

Pink marker: *Faber-Castell GRIP*

TECHNIQUES

Acrylic paint

Paper punching

Drawing or tracing

Lettering

9 I will sing a new song to you, O God;
    upon a ten-stringed harp I will play to you,
10 who gives victory to kings,
    who rescues David his servant from the cruel sword.
11 Rescue me and deliver me
    from the hand of foreigners,
    whose mouths speak lies
    and whose right hand is a right hand of falsehood.

12 May our sons in their youth
    be like plants full grown,
    our daughters like corner pillars
    cut for the structure of a palace;
13 may our granaries be full,
    providing all kinds of produce;
    may our sheep bring forth thousands
    and ten thousands in our fields;
14 may our cattle be heavy with young,
    suffering no mishap or failure in bearing;[1]
    may there be no cry of distress in our streets!
15 Blessed are the people to whom such blessings fall!
    Blessed are the people whose God is the LORD!

Great Is the LORD

145[2] A SONG OF PRAISE. OF DAVID.
1 I will extol you, my God and King,
    and bless your name forever and ever.
2 Every day I will bless you
    and praise your name forever and ever.
3 Great is the LORD, and greatly to be praised,
    and his greatness is unsearchable.

4 One generation shall commend your works to another,
    and shall declare your mighty acts.
5 On the glorious splendor of your majesty,
    and on your wondrous works, I will meditate.
6 They shall speak of the might of your awesome deeds,
    and I will declare your greatness.
7 They shall pour forth the fame of your abundant goodness
    and shall sing aloud of your righteousness.

8 The LORD is gracious and merciful,
    slow to anger and abounding in steadfast love.
9 The LORD is good to all,
    and his mercy is over all that he has made.

10 All your works shall give thanks to you, O LORD,
    and all your saints shall bless you!
11 They shall speak of the glory of your kingdom
    and tell of your power,
12 to make known to the children of man your[3] mighty deeds,
    and the glorious splendor of your kingdom.

[1] Hebrew with no breaking in or going out [2] This psalm is an acrostic poem, each verse beginning with the successive letters of the Hebrew alphabet [3] Hebrew his; also next line

Selah

PSALM 145:12

GOD showers COMPASSION on ALL His Creation

HIS faithful followers will PRAISE HIM & Speak of the GLORY of HIS Kingdom HIS power HIS mighty deeds & HIS majestic reign

1 On a piece of white card stock with a foam brush, paint random strokes of red and pink acrylic paint and allow it to dry.

2 Use a large heart-shaped paper punch to punch out one large heart.

3 With a small heart-shaped punch, punch out multiple small hearts.

TIP
Photocopy your Bible page to practice word placement and then use a light table to trace it into your Bible!

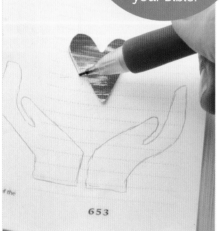

4 With a pencil, sketch out the basic shape of two hands (or trace the hands on page 151) in the bottom of the margin. Place the large punched heart above the hands and lightly trace around it so you know where it will go.

5 With a pencil, trace two concentric circles from page 147. Above the drawing, sketch out the hand lettering of the list you created for these verses. Use bigger or bolder lettering to emphasize important words.

6 Use the black pen to trace over all of the pencil lines and then erase any remaining ones. Add doodles of hearts within the text if desired.

7 With the black pen, create a checkerboard pattern in the circles. Draw small dots around the outside of the large circle with the pen.

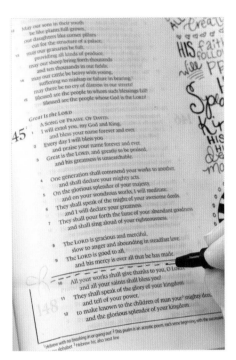

8 Use the black pen, and ruler if desired, to draw a rectangle around the verses.

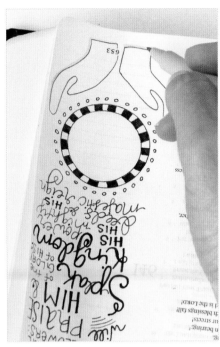

9 With the light gray marker, create a shadow under the hands.

10 Adhere the hearts to the page with the glue stick.

11 Use the pink pen to color in any details on the word art, such as underlining words or filling in doodled hearts.

12 Draw a bow in the upper left corner of the rectangle with the black pen. Shade the bottom edge of the bow and the rectangle with the light gray marker. Inside the rectangle, draw stitch lines with the black pen.

THE LETTER OF
JAMES

Greeting

1 James, a servant[1] of God and of the Lord Jesus Christ,

To the twelve tribes in the Dispersion:

Greetings.

Testing of Your Faith

2 Count it all joy, my brothers,[2] when you meet trials of various kinds, 3 for you know that the testing of your faith produces steadfastness. 4 And let steadfastness have its full effect, that you may be perfect and complete, lacking in nothing. 5 If any of you lacks wisdom, let him ask God, who gives generously to all without reproach, and it will be given him. 6 But let him ask in faith, with no doubting, for the one who doubts is like a wave of the sea that is driven and tossed by the wind. 7 For that person must not suppose that he will receive anything from the Lord; 8 he is a double-minded man, unstable in all his ways.

9 Let the lowly brother boast in his exaltation, 10 and the rich in his humiliation, because like a flower of the grass[3] he will pass away. 11 For the sun rises with its scorching heat and withers the grass; its flower falls, and its beauty perishes. So also will the rich man fade away in the midst of his pursuits.

12 Blessed is the man who remains steadfast under trial, for when he has stood the test he will receive the crown of life, which God has promised to those who love him. 13 Let no one say when he is tempted, "I am being tempted by God," for God cannot be tempted with evil, and he himself tempts no one. 14 But each person is tempted when he is lured and enticed by his own desire. 15 Then desire when it has conceived gives birth to sin, and sin when it is fully grown brings forth death.

16 Do not be deceived, my beloved brothers. 17 Every good gift and every perfect gift is from above, coming down from the Father of lights with whom there is no variation or shadow due to change.[4] 18 Of his own will he brought us forth by the word of truth, that we should be a kind of firstfruits of his creatures.

Hearing and Doing the Word

19 Know this, my beloved brothers: let every person be quick to hear, slow to speak, slow to anger; 20 for the anger of man does not produce the righteousness of God. 21 Therefore put away all filthiness and rampant wickedness and receive with meekness the implanted word, which is able to save your souls.

22 But be doers of the word, and not hearers only, deceiving yourselves. 23 For if anyone is a hearer of the word and not a doer, he is like a man who looks intently at his natural face in a mirror. 24 For he looks at himself and goes away and at once forgets what he was like. 25 But the one who looks into the perfect law, the law of liberty, and perseveres, being no hearer who forgets but a doer who acts, he will be blessed in his doing.

26 If anyone thinks he is religious and does not bridle his tongue but deceives his heart, this person's religion is worthless. 27 Religion that is pure and undefiled before God, the Father, is this: to visit orphans and widows in their affliction, and to keep oneself unstained from the world.

[1] Or slave (for the contextual rendering of the Greek word doulos, see Preface) [2] Or brothers and sisters. The plural Greek word adelphoi (translated "brothers") refers to siblings in a family. In New Testament usage, depending on the context, adelphoi may refer either to men or to both men and women who are siblings (brothers and sisters) in God's family, the church; also verses 16, 19 [3] Or a wild flower [4] Some manuscripts variation due to a shadow of turning

The Sin of Partiality

2 My brothers,[1] show no ... Lord of glory. 2 For if a ... assembly, and a poor man ... to the one who wears the ... you say to the poor man ... not then made distinctio ... 5 Listen, my beloved bro ... be rich in faith and hei ... him? 6 But you have dis ... you, and the ones who ... honorable name by wh ...

8 If you really fulfil ... neighbor as yourself," ... ting sin and are conv ... law but fails in one p ... not commit adultery, ... do murder, you hav ... who are to be judge ... who has shown no ...

Faith Without Wo

14 What good i ... works? Can that ... in daily food, 16 ... without giving ... faith by itself, if ...

18 But someo ... apart from you ... God is one; you ... shown, you foc ... our father jus ... that faith was ... the Scripture ... him as righte ... justified by w ... the prostitu ... out by anoth ... from works ...

Taming th

3 Not m ... who te ... ways. An ... also to b ... obey us, ... are so la ... wherever ... boasts o ...

How ... world ... body, s ... of bea ...

[1] Or brot ... [d] Gen. 1 ...

Fearless Acrylic Painting

JAMES 1:22

For many people, the thought of painting with acrylic paint in their Bible is scary. It's so opaque and permanent. What if they mess it up? I understand those fears because even as a seasoned mixed-media art journaler it definitely made me pause and think about how I should go about applying that beautiful paint to my Bible page. Then I came across a friend's brilliant idea to paint on deli paper and then adhere it to her Bible. I had used deli paper many times in my art journals and loved how the unpainted parts just melt into the layers behind it, so I was excited to try it out. It's now one of the materials I use most often in my Bible journal pages when using paint or similar mediums.

Reading James 1:9–27 led me to think about what type of Christ follower I am. Am I one who just reads, listens to, and art journals God's Word and that's it? Or do I live out the wisdom I've gained from the Bible by being obedient to what God tells me to do in His Word? I want to be a "doer," not just a listener, and apply the truths He has given me to my life. This page is a reminder to do just that.

SUPPLIES

Washi tape: *MT Tape*

Waxed deli paper

Craft mat: *Ranger*

Acrylic paint: *Liquitex* in primary yellow, titanium white, and aqua green; *DecoArt Americana* in bubblegum pink

Palette paper

Scraper (an old credit card can be used)

Texture makers: bubble wrap, punchinella (sequin waste), crumpled paper, etc.

Black card stock

Scissors

Gel medium

Sponge brush

Black pen: *Faber-Castell PITT Artist Pen*

Word art on page 153

Colored pencil: *Prismacolor Premier* in canary yellow or other coordinating color

Pencil

Eraser

TECHNIQUES

Acrylic paint

Creating texture and patterns

1 Adhere a piece of washi tape to the outer edge of the Bible page margin.

TIP
Using a scraper, such as an old credit or key card, allows you to quickly get the paint down on the paper and prevents you from using too much.

2 Lay a piece of deli paper onto a craft mat. A craft mat will protect your work surface from the excess paint. Place a few drops of the acrylic paint onto the palette paper.

3 Use a scraper to pick up some paint off your palette and carefully scrape it across your deli paper.

4 Repeat Step 2 with the other colors to cover about half of the deli paper sheet.

5 Use various texture tools to create patterns with paint. Those items can be dipped into the paint and then pounced onto the deli paper. If using punchinella, lay it onto the paper and then lightly paint over it, as if you're using a stencil. Remove it to reveal the polka dot design.

Creating a Margin Template

It can be useful to have a template of your Bible page margin, especially when working with something like deli paper. You can use it as a guide for the size of your "canvas" and then to cut out the paper to the exact size. Create a margin template by measuring the page height and margin width and cutting a piece of black card stock to those dimensions. Round the outer corners if your Bible has rounded corners.

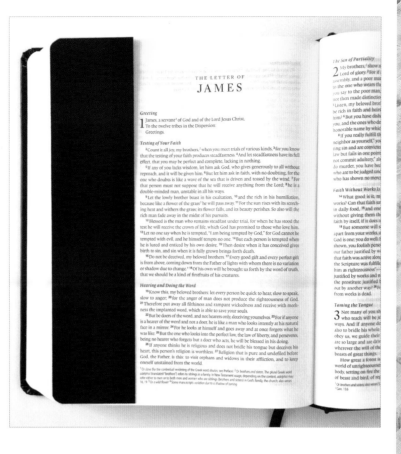

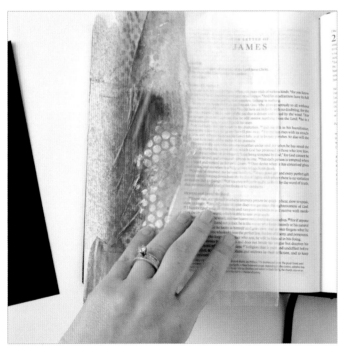

6 Place the painted deli paper on the page, lining it up so that the portion of the design you want to use is in place on the page.

7 Place the margin template over the painted deli paper and then trace around it and cut it out.

8 Apply gel medium to the back of the deli paper with a sponge brush. The gel medium acts as an adhesive.

9 Gently place the deli paper, gel medium side down, on the Bible margin and carefully smooth it. Allow it to dry.

TIP
Feel free to create your own word art, either on the computer and printing or by drawing directly on the deli paper.

10 Lightly color over the corresponding verse with a colored pencil.

11 With a new sheet of deli paper and a black pen, trace over the word art on page 153. Cut around the text on the deli paper with scissors.

12 Apply gel medium to the back side of the deli paper with a sponge brush, adhere it to the Bible margin on top of the painting, and allow it to dry.

13 Using a pencil, sketch three arrows pointing to the verse. Use a black pen to trace over them.

Printing on Deli Paper

The instructions above show you how you can trace over words and use them in your Bible, but if you'd like to print directly onto the deli paper, follow these steps.

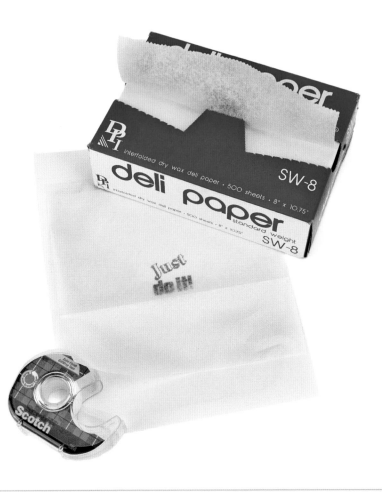

1. On a piece of computer paper, print out the text you'd like to use so you can see exactly where it will appear.

2. Using transparent adhesive tape, tape a piece of deli paper over the text on the computer paper. Pay close attention to adhering the top portion of the deli paper well so it doesn't jam in the printer.

3. Reload the paper into the printer and print it again.

4. Once it has printed and the ink has dried, remove the deli paper from the computer paper.

Secret Journaling

EXODUS 14:13–14

A few years ago, my Bible study fellowship class was studying the life of Moses. We learned how the Egyptians who were in pursuit of the Israelites they had been keeping as slaves were stopped from recapturing them when the Lord parted the Red Sea for His people to cross safely over. When I heard this story, I was struck by how afraid the Israelites must have been. They didn't know that God would miraculously save them. They had to decide to follow the leadership of Moses, who told them not to be afraid. They had to obey God, putting aside all hopelessness and step forward onto that dry ground between the parted waters with utter faith.

Although my troubles and trials may not be that climactic, I do know what hopeless despair feels like. These verses took me back to a time in my life when I was fighting those feelings and how I had to make a decision to trust the Lord or to try to get through it on my own.

I knew that I wanted to art journal about these feelings, but at the same time I didn't want anyone who happened to flip through my Bible to see the personal things I wanted to say to God in prayer. So I wrote out that prayer and tucked it into an envelope!

1 Trace the envelope template on page 149 onto a piece of kraft-colored card stock, cut it out, and fold on the score lines. Use the bone folder to sharpen the folds. Apply adhesive to the bottom tab. Fold in one side of the envelope. Apply adhesive to the inside edge of the other side and fold in the side to complete the envelope.

SUPPLIES

Pencil

Eraser

Envelope template (page 149)

Kraft-colored card stock

Scissors

Bone folder

Adhesive: *Scotch Advanced Tape Glider (ATG)*

Letter stamps: *Adorn It*

Acrylic blocks or *MISTI*

Embossing ink: *Tsukineko VersaMark*

Embossing powder: *Stampendous!* in white

Scratch paper

Craft heat gun

Gel pen: *Signo* in white

"Trust God" sticker (from sticker sheet at back of book)

Washi tape: *Stampin' Up! Recollections*

Word art (page 153; optional)

Light box or tablet device with light box app (optional)

Watercolor pencil: *Faber-Castell Art GRIP Aquarelle* in light blue

Water brush

Black pen: *Faber-Castell PITT Artist Pen* (small and medium nibs)

Adhesive *Velcro* tab (optional)

TECHNIQUES

Stamping

Embossing

Lettering or tracing

Watercolor pencils

[10]When Pharaoh drew near, the people of Israel lifted up their eyes, and behold, the Egyptians were marching after them, and they feared greatly. And the people of Israel cried out to the LORD. [11]They said to Moses, "Is it because there are no graves in Egypt that you have taken us away to die in the wilderness? What have you done to us in bringing us out of Egypt? [12]Is not this what we said to you in Egypt: 'Leave us alone that we may serve the Egyptians'? For it would have been better for us to serve the Egyptians than to die in the wilderness." [13]And Moses said to the people, "Fear not, stand firm, and see the salvation of the LORD, which he will work for you today. For the Egyptians whom you see today, you shall never see again. [14]The LORD will fight for you, and you have only to be silent."

[15]The LORD said to Moses, "Why do you cry to me? Tell the people of Israel to go forward. [16]Lift up your staff, and stretch out your hand over the sea and divide it, that the people of Israel may go through the sea on dry ground. [17]And I will harden the hearts of the Egyptians so that they shall go in after them, and I will get glory over Pharaoh and all his host, his chariots, and his horsemen. [18]And the Egyptians shall know that I am the LORD, when I have gotten glory over Pharaoh, his chariots, and his horsemen."

[19]Then the angel of God who was going before the host of Israel moved and went behind them, and the pillar of cloud moved from before them and stood behind them, [20]coming between the host of Egypt and the host of Israel. And there was the cloud and the darkness. And it lit up the night[1] without one coming near the other all night.

[21]Then Moses stretched out his hand over the sea, and the LORD drove the sea back by a strong east wind all night and made the sea dry land, and the waters were divided. [22]And the people of Israel went into the midst of the sea on dry ground, the waters being a wall to them on their right hand and on their left. [23]The Egyptians pursued and went in after them into the midst of the sea, all Pharaoh's horses, his chariots, and

LET YOUR
Faith
BE BIGGER THAN
your
fear

FEAR NOT
stand firm
TRUST GOD

65

2 Choose the letter stamps that spell "Fear Not" and place them onto the acrylic block, ink them with embossing ink, and then stamp them onto the envelope. See page 51 for instructions on using the MISTI.

3 Sprinkle the embossing powder onto the stamped words and tap it off onto a piece of scratch paper. Use a heat gun about 8–10" (20–25 cm) away from the envelope to melt the embossing powder. Allow the embossing to cool.

4 Under the stamped text, hand write "stand firm" with a pencil and then trace over it with a white gel pen. After it's dry, erase any visible pencil lines.

TIP
Gel pens take a little time to dry. As you're working, be careful not to drag your hand over your work, which might smear it.

5 Using a pencil, sketch an arrow under "stand firm." Place the "trust God" sticker under the arrow. With the white gel pen, trace over the arrow and then doodle on the envelope flap as desired.

6 Tear off a strip of turquoise washi tape and adhere half of it to the left edge of the envelope. Adhere the envelope to the center of your Bible.

7 Adhere a strip of black washi tape and trim if necessary.

8 Trace the word art (from page 153) onto the Bible page or sketch your design. Color in the design using a watercolor pencil and then activate it by painting it in with a water brush. (See page 80 for tips on working with watercolor pencils.)

9 After the watercolor is dry, trace over the pencil lines with the black pens. Use the small nib for fine lines and the medium nib for thicker letters.

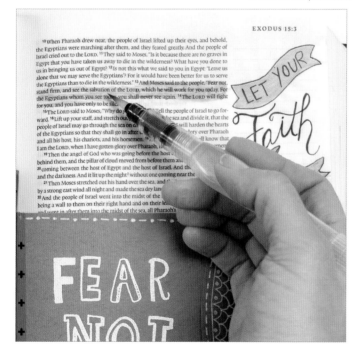

10 Color in the scripture passage with the watercolor pencil, then activate it with the water brush.

11 Tuck a prayer or other memento into the envelope. Seal the envelope or just tuck the flap in or apply adhesive Velcro under the envelope flap to keep it closed.

just wait

on *the* **LORD**

10 who say t
and to
speak to u
proph

11 leave the
let us h

12 Therefore
"Because y
and tru
and rel

13 therefore
like a b
whose
collapse,

14 and its br
that is
that amo
with w
or to di

15 For thus s
"In returni
in quietness and in trust shall be your strength."
But you were unwilling, 16 and you said,
"No! We will flee upon horses";
therefore you shall flee away;
and, "We will ride upon swift steeds";
therefore your pursuers shall be swift.

17 A thousand shall flee at the threat of one;
at the threat of five you shall flee,
till you are left
like a flagstaff on the top of a mountain,
like a signal on a hill.

The LORD Will Be Gracious

18 Therefore the LORD waits to be gracious to you,
and therefore he exalts himself to show mercy to you.
For the LORD is a God of justice;
blessed are all those who wait for him.

19 For a people shall dwell in Zion, in Jerusalem; you shall weep no more. He will surely be gracious to you at the sound of your cry. As soon as he hears it, he answers you. 20 And though the Lord give you the bread of adversity and the water of affliction, yet your Teacher will not hide himself anymore, but your eyes shall see your Teacher. 21 And your ears shall hear a word behind you, saying, "This is the way, walk in it," when you turn to the right or when you turn to the left. 22 Then you will defile your carved idols overlaid with silver and your gold-plated metal images. You will scatter them as unclean things. You will say to them, "Be gone!"

23 And he will give rain for the seed with which you sow the ground, and bread, the produce of the ground, which will be rich and plenteous. In that day your livestock will graze in large pastures, 24 and the oxen and the donkeys that work the ground will eat seasoned fodder, which has been winnowed with shovel and fork. 25 And on every lofty mountain and every high hill there will be brooks running with water, in the day of the great slaughter, when the towers fall. 26 Moreover, the light of the moon will be

¹ Or *repentance*

Faithbooking

ISAIAH 30:18

I'd venture to say that most of us have things in our life that we have had to wait for. If you're familiar with my story from reading my blog or you know me in "real life," you know that my husband and I struggle with God's timing in building our family. It's been a hard road, but we trust that He knows better than we do what the big picture for our lives looks like.

I came across Isaiah 30:18 and it jumped out at me. I saw the graciousness of God's everlasting love that He desires to give us in spite of ourselves or our circumstances. It dawned on me that in my rush to stop waiting I may be missing treasures in His Word and in the life that He has given me.

I decided to use scrapbooking supplies to create an image that fits the theme—a clock, naturally! Supplies made for scrapbooking provide a wide assortment of printed papers, stickers, and other materials that are often coordinated, making it easy to create a cohesive design. But I wanted to personalize it with my own thoughts on waiting on the Lord, so I jotted them down on a sticky note.

SUPPLIES

Scrapbooking kit: *Simple Stories "The Reset Girl"*

Scissors or die-cutting machine

Glue stick

Letter stickers: *Studio Calico* in gray, *Lilly Bee Designs* in pink, and *Simple Stories* in green

Ruler

Black pen: Faber-Castell PITT Artist Pen (small nib)

Sticky notes: *Simple Stories "Planner Girl"*

Washi tape: *Simple Stories "Planner Girl"*

TECHNIQUES

Paper crafting

Letter stickers

Sticky Situation

If you're intimidated to art journal in your Bible, a great way to start adding your thoughts or doodles is to put them on removable sticky notes. It's also an easy way to add to your page without permanently covering up any scripture.

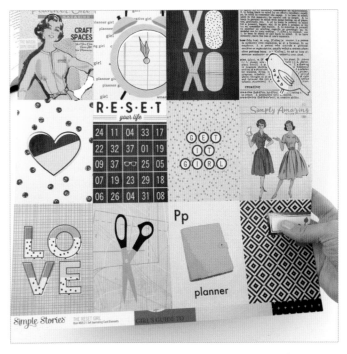

1 Find the 3 x 4 Journaling Card Elements paper in the scrapbooking kit.

2 Cut out the clock in two pieces: the clock base and the alarm bell sections.

3 Using a glue stick, adhere the clock to the center of the page margin, properly spacing the two sections.

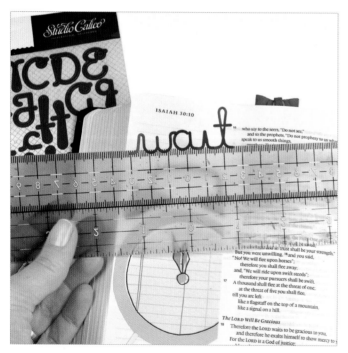

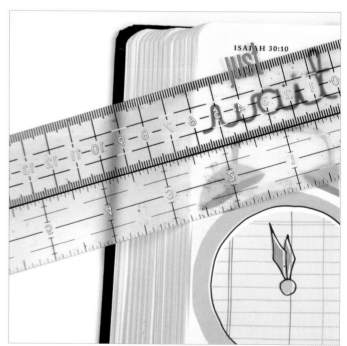

4 Remove the gray letters to spell "wait" and place them onto the edge of a ruler so just the bottom edge of the stickers are stuck to the ruler. Place the ruler on top of the page where you want the word to go and press down firmly on the stickers with one hand as you gently pull out the ruler with the other hand.

5 Place pink letters onto the ruler in the same manner to spell out "just" and then adhere it above the word "wait." Place pink letters onto the ruler in the same manner to spell out "on" and adhere it under the clock to the right of the clock's foot.

6 Place the green letters onto the ruler in the same manner to spell out "Lord" and adhere them under the word "on." Use a black pen to handwrite the word "the" next to "on."

7 On one of the sticky notes from the kit, journal your thoughts and then add it to your page in the upper margin.

8 Dress up your sticky note by adding a strip of green washi tape to the top of it and then layer a pink strip of washi tape over that. You can cut the tape lengthwise if you would like it to be narrower.

9 Add a heart sticker from the kit to the sticky note. Use an arrow sticker from the kit to point to the verse.

Photo Journaling

GENESIS 2:24

As an avid picture taker and scrapbooker, I often come across meaningful photos that I want to include in my Bible. Now of course I could add them as is into my Bible, but I usually try not to obscure the scripture in my journal pages. I realized that by printing a photo on a clear transparency, I could incorporate it into my journaling Bible, but still see the scripture passages behind it.

I recently heard a sermon about marriage and decided to create a page on Genesis 2:24 in which Moses tell us about God establishing marriage. This verse tells us some essential things about a couple's union. They should be independent of their families and dependent on each other, being joined together permanently as one flesh. Not having any ephemera left over from my wedding seventeen years ago, I chose one of the photos from our special day to use. I thought that a pretty, white paper doily would evoke similar feelings and would be the perfect surface on which to display lettering from the verse.

SUPPLIES

Computer

Transparency film: *Apollo Quick-Dry Ink Jet Printer Transparency Film* (make sure the film is compatible with your printer)

Printer

Sharpie

Paper trimmer or scissors

6" (15 cm) white paper doily

Word art (page 153; optional)

Light box or tablet device with light box app (optional)

Black pen: *Tombow Fudenosuke Brush Pen*

Adhesive: *Scotch Advanced Tape Glider (ATG)*

TECHNIQUES

Printing on transparency film

Lettering or tracing

More Ways to Incorporate Photos

Photographs, especially of friends and loved ones, are such personal images that they can create very meaningful additions to your Bible pages. Here are a few more ways in which you can journal with them.

- **Adhere a photo to a slightly larger piece of card stock or patterned paper and tape into your Bible with washi tape as a tip-in.**

- **If it is small enough to fit into your margin or if you don't mind covering some wording, adhere the photo directly to the Bible page with adhesive (such as Scotch Advanced Tape Glider).**

- **Fussy cut (see page 68) around an image to create an embellishment to attach to your page.**

- **Slip a photo into your Bible as a bookmark.**

TIP
Keep in mind that the transparency's printed side will go against the Bible page, while the smooth side will face up.

1 In a photo-editing program, flip your image so that it is the mirror image of how you want it to appear in the Bible. Print the photo onto the transparency using the manufacturer's instructions. Allow the transparency to dry thoroughly. If the transparency you used has a removable sensing strip, remove it.

2 Place your transparency onto your Bible page to decide where it needs to be trimmed. With a Sharpie, mark where you want to cut at the edge of the transparency.

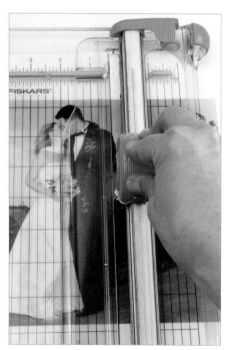

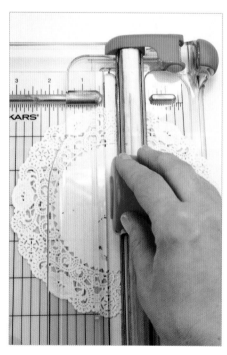

3 Use a paper trimmer or scissors to trim the transparency.

4 Cut the doily in half with scissors or a paper trimmer.

5 Add lettering to the doily or trace the word art from page 153 with the black pen.

6 Apply adhesive to the back of the doily along the cut edge.

7 Adhere the doily to the transparency.

8 Apply adhesive down the back left edge of the transparency.

9 Adhere it to the page gutter.

in Jesus THERE IS **FREEDOM** *NO CONDEMNATION*

what I do not want, I agree with the law, that it is good. ¹⁷ So now it is no longer I who do it, but sin that dwells within me. ¹⁸ For I know that nothing good dwells in me, that is, in my flesh. For I have the desire to do what is right, but not the ability to carry it out. ¹⁹ For I do not do the good I want, but the evil I do not want is what I keep on doing. ²⁰ Now if I do what I do not want, it is no longer I who do it, but sin that dwells within me.

²¹ So I find it to be a law that when I want to do right, evil lies close at hand. ²² For I delight in the law of God, in my inner being, ²³ but I see in my members another law waging war against the law of my mind and making me captive to the law of sin that dwells in my members. ²⁴ Wretched man that I am! Who will deliver me from this body of death? ²⁵ Thanks be to God through Jesus Christ our Lord! So then, I myself serve the law of God with my mind, but with my flesh I serve the law of sin.

life in the spirit

8 There is therefore now no condemnation for those who are in Christ Jesus.[1] ² For the law of the Spirit of life has set you[2] free in Christ Jesus from the law of sin and death. ³ For God has done what the law, weakened by the flesh, could not do. By sending his own Son in the likeness of sinful flesh and for sin,[3] he condemned sin in the flesh, ⁴ in order that the righteous requirement of the law might be fulfilled in us, who walk not according to the flesh but according to the Spirit. ⁵ For those who live according to the flesh set their minds on the things of the flesh, but those who live according to the Spirit set their minds on the things of the Spirit. ⁶ For to set the mind on the flesh is death, but to set the mind on the Spirit is life and peace. ⁷ For the mind that is set on the flesh is hostile to God, for it does not submit to God's law; indeed, it cannot. ⁸ Those who are in the flesh cannot please God.

⁹ You, however, are not in the flesh but in the Spirit, if in fact the Spirit of God dwells in you. Anyone who does not have the Spirit of Christ does not belong to him. ¹⁰ But if Christ is in you, although the body is dead because of sin, the Spirit is life because of righteousness. ¹¹ If the Spirit of him who raised Jesus from the dead dwells in you, he who raised Christ Jesus[4] from the dead will also give life to your mortal bodies through his Spirit who dwells in you.

Heirs with Christ

¹² So then, brothers,[5] we are debtors, not to the flesh, to live according to the flesh. ¹³ For if you live according to the flesh you will die, but if by the Spirit you put to death the deeds of the body, you will live. ¹⁴ For all who are led by the Spirit of God are sons[6] of God. ¹⁵ For you did not receive the spirit of slavery to fall back into fear, but you have received the Spirit of adoption as sons, by whom we cry, "Abba! Father!" ¹⁶ The Spirit himself bears witness with our spirit that we are children of God, ¹⁷ and if children, then heirs—heirs of God and fellow heirs with Christ, provided we suffer with him in order that we may also be glorified with him.

Future Glory

¹⁸ For I consider that the sufferings of this present time are not worth comparing with the glory that is to be revealed to us. ¹⁹ For the creation waits with eager longing for the revealing of the sons of God. ²⁰ For the creation was subjected to futility, not willingly, but because of him who subjected it, in hope ²¹ that the creation itself will be set free from its bondage to corruption and obtain the freedom of the glory of the children of God. ²² For we know that the whole creation has been groaning together in the pains of childbirth until now. ²³ And not only the creation, but we ourselves, who have the firstfruits of the Spirit, groan inwardly as we wait eagerly for adoption as sons, the redemption of our bodies. ²⁴ For in this hope we were saved. Now hope that is seen is not hope. For who hopes for what he sees? ²⁵ But if we hope for what we do not see, we wait for it with patience.

¹ Some manuscripts add who walk not according to the flesh (but according to the Spirit) ² Some manuscripts me ³ Or and as a sin offering ⁴ Some manuscripts lack Jesus ⁵ Or brothers and sisters; also verse 29 ⁶ See discussion on "sons" in the Preface

---

²⁶ Likewise t... as we ought, b... ²⁷ And he who... intercedes for... who love God... to his purpose... to the image of... ³⁰ And those... justified, and...

God's Everla...

³¹ What th... us? ³² He wh... also with hi... God's elect?... died—mor... interceding... distress, or p...

³⁷ No, in all... I am sure th... to come, no... able to sep...

God's Sov...

9 I am s... in the... ³ For I cou... my broth... belong to t... the promi... flesh, is t...

⁶ But it... from Isr... offsprin... not the c... ise are c... year I w... had com... born ar... might... ⁴ "The... ¹⁴ W... says to... on wh... but to... I have... be rob... hard...

rejoice Christ ligh

Creating Embellishments

ROMANS 8:1–11

Verses 1–11 of Romans chapter 8 talk about how those who belong to Jesus are not condemned for our sin because the Holy Spirit is living. There is nothing we can do to earn God's forgiveness. His overwhelming grace is the only way. We can't just be good people, or give money, or anything else to belong to Jesus. We just trust Him in faith, and His amazing grace covers our sins.

I didn't want to detract from this crucial message, so I kept the page pretty simple. I highlighted the key verse, then placed letter stickers above it to express the theme for that section of scripture. I then created a bookmark to go on the page. The word art that is on the bookmark could have been added to the margin, or I could have used the bookmark in the traditional way instead of attaching it to the page, but I liked the way combining the two ideas added some diversity to the page.

SUPPLIES

Bookmark (from the die-cut sheet at the back of this book)

Washi tapes: *Documented Faith*; *Simple Stories*; *Scotch*

Scissors

Black pens: *Faber-Castell PITT Artist Pens* (small and medium nibs)

Marker: *Tombow Jelly Bean Collection* in pink

Pencil

Eraser

Mouse pad or foam

Paper piercer or thin nail

Black brad: *Doodlebug*

Sticky notes: *Post-It* (optional)

Letter stickers: *Cosmo Cricket*

TECHNIQUES

Letter stickers

Making a bookmark

More Ideas for Embellishments

Embellishments add a three-dimensional element to your page that can really pop. Attach them with adhesive, such as Scotch Advanced Tape Glider, washi tape, a brad, or staple them to the page. Here are some more ways to make your own:

- Create bookmarks similar to the one shown with this project by cutting out and coloring the black-and-white margin art in the Bonus Art section at the back of the book.

- Stamp images onto card stock, cut them out, and adhere them to the page.

- Create your own painted papers and cut or punch out shapes to add to your margins (see Steps 1 and 2 on page 106).

- Layer multiple purchased embellishments, such as tip-ins and stickers, to create your own design.

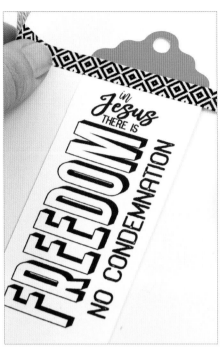

1 Remove the bookmark from the sheet of die-cut images at the back of the book. Cut a piece of magenta washi tape and adhere it to the top of the front of the tag. Trim off the excess.

2 Adhere a smaller piece of black-and-white geometric washi tape under the magenta and trim it as well.

3 Adhere two pieces of washi tape underneath the text. Trim off the bottom of the tag below the washi tape.

4 Take the piece you removed from the bottom of the tag, place it over the bottom edge, and use it as a template to cut a new "dove's tail" at the bottom of the tag.

5 Using the small-tipped black pen, draw a short horizontal line on both sides of the phrase "no condemnation." Use a pink marker to add little dots above and below the lines.

6 Place your bookmark on your Bible page and use a pencil to mark where to place the hole for the brad.

7 Place a mouse pad or other soft surface underneath the Bible page and use a paper piercer or thin nail to poke a hole where you marked.

8 Place the brad through the bookmark hole and then through the hole in the page. Turn the page over and open the legs of the brad.

9 To protect the verses you don't want colored, place sticky notes over them. Use a pink pen to color the verse.

10 Place letter stickers above the highlighted verse to write out "life in the spirit."

Monoprinting

ROMANS 8:31–39

Verses 31–39 in Romans chapter 8 discuss the eternal security Believers experience in Christ. Jesus died, was resurrected, and is now sitting at the right hand of God interceding for us. He did all that because of His love for us. His love for us, not ours for Him, is what makes it impossible for anything in all of creation to separate us from that unconditional love.

When I think about love and which colors I want to use to represent it, I think of the traditional red and pink we associate with Valentine's Day. I wanted to create a vibrant painted border around the page on which I could add doodles and other embellishments. To do this I painted on a Gelli Arts Gel Printing Plate with a stencil, acrylic paints, and texture tools. I then created a "monoprint" on deli paper. As the name implies, a monoprint is usually a single print, but I printed several other papers with the same gel plate. The more prints you make in this way, the less vibrant they are, but they still add wonderful color and texture to your Bible pages.

I concentrated on God's everlasting love by creating some word art in the margin. As I created it, I really meditated as I doodled about the fact that nothing can separate me from His love and it left me thanking Him with overwhelming gratitude.

Prints Charming

Steps 1–6 of this project explain how to create gorgeously colored and textured papers to decorate your Bible art journal pages. You can repeat these steps using various stencils and mark-making tools. The possibilities are endless! While you have your Gelli Arts Gel Printing Plate and all your supplies out, make a batch of deli papers you can use in various projects.

This book also includes a sheet of vellum printed with a few of my painted patterns that can be cut out and used in the same way as your painted deli papers.

SUPPLIES

Gelli Arts Gel Printing Plate

Acrylic paint: Liquitex in purple, pink, and red; DecoArt Americana in light buttermilk

Brayer

Palette paper

Texture tools: bottle lids, bubble wrap, corrugated cardboard, etc.

Stencil: Stencil Girl "Peacock"

Waxed deli paper

Scissors or paper trimmer

Glue stick

Washi tape: Documented Life

Black pen: Faber-Castell PITT Artist Pen

Ruler (optional)

Word art (page 153)

Gel medium

Sponge brush

Bone folder

White gel pen: Signo

Pencil

Eraser

Lid (about 2½"/6.5 cm)

TECHNIQUES

Acrylic paint

Stenciling

Texture making

Monoprinting

Doodling

26 Likewise the Spirit helps us in our weakness. For we do not know what to pray for as we ought, but the Spirit himself intercedes for us with groanings too deep for words. 27 And he who searches hearts knows what is the mind of the Spirit, because[1] the Spirit intercedes for the saints according to the will of God. 28 And we know that for those who love God all things work together for good,[2] for those who are called according to his purpose. 29 For those whom he foreknew he also predestined to be conformed to the image of his Son, in order that he might be the firstborn among many brothers. 30 And those whom he predestined he also called, and those whom he called he also justified, and those whom he justified he also glorified.

God's Everlasting Love

31 What then shall we say to these things? If God is for us, who can be[3] against us? 32 He who did not spare his own Son but gave him up for us all, how will he not also with him graciously give us all things? 33 Who shall bring any charge against God's elect? It is God who justifies. 34 Who is to condemn? Christ Jesus is the one who died—more than that, who was raised—who is at the right hand of God, who indeed is interceding for us.[4] 35 Who shall separate us from the love of Christ? Shall tribulation, or distress, or persecution, or famine, or nakedness, or danger, or sword? 36 As it is written,

"For your sake we are being killed all the day long;
    we are regarded as sheep to be slaughtered."

37 No, in all these things we are more than conquerors through him who loved us. 38 For I am sure that neither death nor life, nor angels nor rulers, nor things present nor things to come, nor powers, 39 nor height nor depth, nor anything else in all creation, will be able to separate us from the love of God in Christ Jesus our Lord.

God's Sovereign Choice

9 I am speaking the truth in Christ—I am not lying; my conscience bears me witness in the Holy Spirit— 2 that I have great sorrow and unceasing anguish in my heart. 3 For I could wish that I myself were accursed and cut off from Christ for the sake of my brothers,[5] my kinsmen according to the flesh. 4 They are Israelites, and to them belong the adoption, the glory, the covenants, the giving of the law, the worship, and the promises. 5 To them belong the patriarchs, and from their race, according to the flesh, is the Christ, who is God over all, blessed forever. Amen.

6 But it is not as though the word of God has failed. For not all who are descended from Israel belong to Israel, 7 and not all are children of Abraham because they are his offspring, but ^b"Through Isaac shall your offspring be named." 8 This means that it is not the children of the flesh who are the children of God, but the children of the promise are counted as offspring. 9 For this is what the promise said: ^c"About this time next year I will return, and Sarah shall have a son." 10 And not only so, but also when Rebekah had conceived children by one man, our forefather Isaac, 11 though they were not yet born and had done nothing either good or bad—in order that God's purpose of election might continue, not because of works but because of him who calls— 12 she was told, ^d"The older will serve the younger." 13 As it is written, "Jacob I loved, but Esau I hated."

14 What shall we say then? Is there injustice on God's part? By no means! 15 For he says to Moses, ^f"I will have mercy on whom I have mercy, and I will have compassion on whom I have compassion." 16 So then it depends not on human will or exertion,[6] but on God, who has mercy. 17 For the Scripture says to Pharaoh, ^g"For this very purpose I have raised you up, that I might show my power in you, and that my name might be proclaimed in all the earth." 18 So then he has mercy on whomever he wills, and he hardens whomever he wills.

absolutely NOTHING can separate Me FROM His LOVE

i am grateful   i am loved

i am lov   i am forgiven

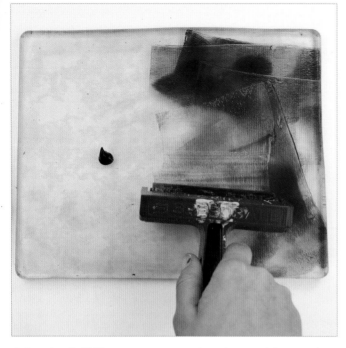

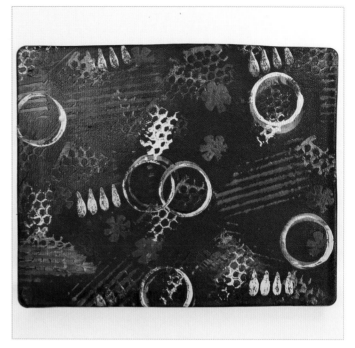

1 Lay the Gelli Plate onto your work surface and then squirt a few dollops of purple acrylic paint randomly onto it. Use the brayer to spread it all over the Gelli Plate.

2 Put some red and pink acrylic paint onto palette paper, dip various texture tools into the paint colors, and then tap them over the Gelli plate.

3 Place a stencil over the Gelli Plate. Squirt a few dollops of pink acrylic paint onto the palette and run the brayer through it until it has a sufficient amount of paint on it. Run the brayer over the stencil.

4 Remove the stencil.

5 Cover the Gelli Plate with a piece of deli paper, pressing it down to pick up the paint. Remove the deli paper and allow to dry.

6 Place more deli papers onto the Gelli Plate. Rub the brayer over them to transfer the remaining paint onto the deli paper. Remove the deli papers and let them dry.

7 Choose one or two of the dry painted pieces of deli paper to go in the top, bottom, and side margins of the page and then cut them to fit there with scissors or a paper trimmer. You can piece portions of the deli paper together if they are not long enough to fit.

8 Apply glue to the back of the deli papers and adhere them to the margins. Allow the page to dry.

9 Take a piece of washi tape that is the width of the Bible page and place it underneath the scripture at the bottom of the page.

10 Use the black pen to draw dashed lines around verses 31–39 using a ruler, if necessary.

11 Trace the word art from page 153 onto a piece of deli paper. Paint just a tiny bit of cream-colored acrylic over the word "from" on the back of the paper. This will make it stand out.

12 Apply gel medium to the back of the deli paper with a sponge brush. Gently place the deli paper, gel medium side down, on the Bible margin and carefully smooth it with a bone folder. Allow it to dry.

13 Use a white gel pen to color in the word "nothing."

14 Using a pencil, trace a lid or cup to make a large circle around the word art. This pencil mark will help you eyeball where to place the doodling.

15 Start by drawing dots along the pencil line with a white pen and then outline the dots with the black pen. Use the black pen to draw a scalloped arc around the dots.

16 Next, draw two parallel arcs above and below the scalloped arcs. Create a checkerboard pattern within them using black and white pens.

Is your Bible getting full? Mine is, and sometimes it takes creative thinking to figure out how to create separate pages that are next to each other. Of course, you can treat them as individuals and do something completely different on each one, but you can also use common elements and colors on both pages to give the spread a cohesive look, as I did here.

celebrating daily life.

15 As for man, his days are like grass;
he flourishes like a flower of the field;
16 for the wind passes over it, and it is gone,
and its place knows it no more.
17 But the steadfast love of the LORD is from everlasting to everlasting
on those who fear him,
and his righteousness to children's children,
18 to those who keep his covenant
and remember to do his commandments.
19 The LORD has established his throne in the heavens,
and his kingdom rules over all.

20 Bless the LORD, O you his angels,
you mighty ones who do his word,
obeying the voice of his word!
21 Bless the LORD, all his hosts,
his ministers, who do his will!
22 Bless the LORD, all his works,
in all places of his dominion.
Bless the LORD, O my soul!

O Lord My God, You Are Very Great

104
1 Bless the LORD, O my soul!
O LORD my God, you are very great!
You are clothed with splendor and majesty,
2 covering yourself with light as with a garment,
stretching out the heavens like a tent.
3 He lays the beams of his chambers on the waters;
he makes the clouds his chariot;
he rides on the wings of the wind;
4 he makes his messengers winds,
his ministers a flaming fire.

5 He set the earth on its foundations,
so that it should never be moved.
6 You covered it with the deep as with a garment;
the waters stood above the mountains.
7 At your rebuke they fled;
at the sound of your thunder they took to flight.
8 The mountains rose, the valleys sank down
to the place that you appointed for them.
9 You set a boundary that they may not pass,
so that they might not again cover the earth.

10 You make springs gush forth in the valleys;
they flow between the hills;
11 they give drink to every beast of the field;
the wild donkeys quench their thirst.
12 Beside them the birds of the heavens dwell;
they sing among the branches.
13 From your lofty abode you water the mountains;
the earth is satisfied with the fruit of your work.

Celebrating Nature

PSALM 104

I love nature, and I don't mean just a little bit. I'm a hiking, tent camping, outdoorsy girl! Being out in nature and seeing how magnificently designed it is gives me such a close feeling of connection with the Lord. I'm forever grateful for His creation, so when I came across Psalm 104 praising God for the creation of the Earth, I knew I wanted to journal about it. And what better way to celebrate nature than to add real bits of it to the page, with dried flowers. It's such an incredibly simple way to create a stunning page.

Dried flowers aren't very flat, so they will add some chunkiness to your Bible; however, they do compress over time. Initially after you create the page it may be harder to create subsequent pages on top of it due to the lumpiness, although you can place a piece of chipboard under those pages when you're creating them.

Don't let all that scare you, though, if you're a nature person, too. If you feel led to honor God by using what He's created, then by all means do so. Every time you see that page you will be reminded of His power to bring it into existence and praise Him for it.

SUPPLIES

Dried flowers and leaves: *LarkspurHill* on Etsy

Tweezers

Camera (optional)

Pencil

Eraser

Black pen: *Faber-Castell PITT Artist Pen* (small nib)

Adhesive: *Tombo Mono Multi Liquid Glue*

Weight (jar or other small, flat-bottomed heavy object)

Stamp: *Technique Tuesday "Simple Joy by Ali Edwards"*

Acrylic block

Black ink: *Tsukineko StazOn*

TECHNIQUES

Using dried flowers

Stamping

More Ways to Celebrate God's Creation

Adding real flowers and leaves to your Bible pages is a very direct way to incorporate nature into your designs. Here are a few more ideas:

- **Stamp with nature-inspired designs, such as flowers, trees, birds, and other animals.**

- **Draw or paint images directly onto your page. See page 27 for tips on drawing flowers.**

- **There are many beautiful stencils of flowers, animals, and other nature motifs that make it easy to create overall patterns or smaller images.**

- **If you're a nature lover like me, you probably have lots of photos you've taken of flowers and landscapes. See Photo Journaling (page 122) for several ways to incorporate photos into your Bible.**

- **Embellish your pages with nature-themed washi tape.**

1 Carefully arrange the dried flowers and leaves onto the margins. Using tweezers is helpful! Take a photograph to remember how they are arranged, then remove them from the Bible page.

2 Use a pencil to draw a bracket in each margin alongside the verses, then trace it with the black pen.

TIP
If a petal or leaf breaks, don't throw it out! Just reassemble the pieces and glue it onto the page. You won't notice it was broken.

3 Apply glue to the back of the flower or leaf and place it where you want it to go.

4 Place a heavy weight on top of the pieces that need help lying flat. I find that a full jar of paint or other material works perfectly.

5 Place the stamp onto the acrylic block, apply ink to it, and stamp it at the top of the page.

I sometimes like to create a journal design that incorporates an entire spread (two pages). Each time I open to these pages and see colorful flowers and leaves, it makes me smile.

Rub-On Letters

SONG OF SOLOMON 2:4

The Song of Solomon is a beautiful depiction of the love between King Solomon and a Shulamite woman—their courtship, the early days of their marriage, and their maturing as a couple. It can be interpreted as showing God's love for His people. One of my favorite verses in this book of the Bible is in chapter 2, verse 4, in which the woman tells of her desire for King Solomon to show how much he loves her by raising a banner over her. In those days, banners or flags identified troops and indicated that they were the possession of a certain country or family and had their protection. The Shulamite woman probably felt such peace having a banner over her, covering her with his love.

I'm so glad that the Lord covers us with a banner of love that is unfailing and eternal. There is nothing that I can do to deserve His love and nothing I can do to diminish or stop His love; I am eternally secure.

When I was designing this page, I thought about how to capture the feelings I had when I was engaged and desiring that love from my beloved. A pendant banner seemed like the perfect depiction of it. I chose rub-on letters because I love how they appear to be printed on the page. Rub-ons are available in a huge variety of images and colors. I chose gold rub-ons because they make the page feel special.

SUPPLIES

Patterned papers: *My Mind's Eye "Everyone Has a Story to Tell"* 6" x 6" (15 x 15 cm) pad

Paper trimmer or scissors

Glue stick: *Xyron*

Rub-on letters: *Ranger*

Bone folder or craft stick

Heart stickers: *Paper Studio*

Black pen: *Faber-Castell PITT Artist Pen* (small nib)

Arrow sticker: *Paper Studio*

TECHNIQUES

Paper crafting

Rub-on letters

Point It Out!

When I choose a passage of scripture to journal about, I like to highlight it, so I remember what I was thinking about and feeling as I created my design. There are a number to do this:

- **Use a highlighter!**
- **Color in the passage with colored pencil, crayon, or a light-colored marker.**
- **Circle the words with a fine-tip pen.**
- **For a longer passage, draw a bracket alongside the lines.**
- **Draw an arrow or add an arrow sticker to point to the scripture.**

10 Your cheeks are lovely with ornaments,
   your neck with strings of jewels.

OTHERS

11 We will make for you[1] ornaments of gold,
   studded with silver.

SHE

12 While the king was on his couch,
   my nard gave forth its fragrance.
13 My beloved is to me a sachet of myrrh
   that lies between my breasts.
14 My beloved is to me a cluster of henna blossoms
   in the vineyards of Engedi.

HE

15 Behold, you are beautiful, my love;
   behold, you are beautiful;
   your eyes are doves.

SHE

16 Behold, you are beautiful, my beloved, truly delightful.
   Our couch is green;
17 the beams of our house are cedar;
   our rafters are pine.

2 ¹ I am a rose[2] of Sharon,
   a lily of the valleys.

HE

2 As a lily among brambles,
   so is my love among the young women.

SHE

3 As an apple tree among the trees of the forest,
   so is my beloved among the young men.
   With great delight I sat in his shadow,
   and his fruit was sweet to my taste.
4 He brought me to the banqueting house,[3]
   and his banner over me was love.
5 Sustain me with raisins;
   refresh me with apples,
   for I am sick with love.
6 His left hand is under my head,
   and his right hand embraces me!
7 I adjure you,[4] O daughters of Jerusalem,
   by the gazelles or the does of the field,
   that you not stir up or awaken love
   until it pleases.

The Bride Adores Her Beloved

8 The voice of my beloved!
   Behold, he comes,

[1] The Hebrew for you is feminine singular [2] Probably a bulb, such as a crocus, asphodel, or narcissus [3] Hebrew the house of wine
[4] That is, I put you on oath; so throughout the Song

HIS BANNER OVER ME IS LOVE

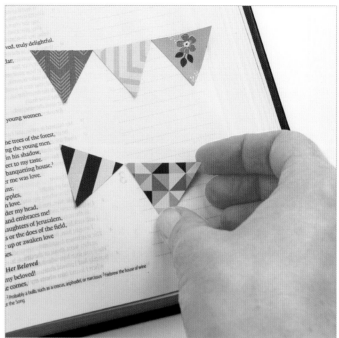

1 Decide which patterned papers you want to use and then cut 10 triangles roughly 1" x 1" (2.5 x 2.5 cm) each with scissors or a paper trimmer.

2 Lay the triangles on the Bible page and arrange them so they look like banners. Be sure to leave enough space for wording to fit. Use a glue stick to adhere the banners. Trim off any pieces that overhang the page.

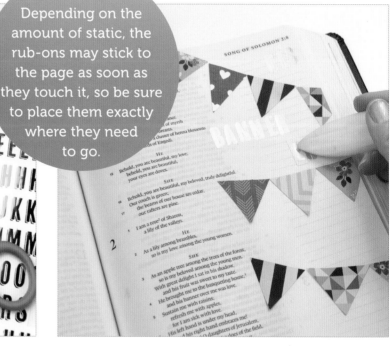

TIP
Depending on the amount of static, the rub-ons may stick to the page as soon as they touch it, so be sure to place them exactly where they need to go.

3 Keeping the backing on, cut out the rub-on letters needed for the words "His banner over me is love." It's really important to keep the backing on so that the letters don't come off the sheet until you're ready for them to. Lay the cut-out letters on the page to determine where they should go,

4 Starting with one letter, remove the backing, being careful not to touch the actual letter. Place it where you want it to go. Using a bone folder or craft stick, rub over the letter. Slowly remove the sheet it was adhered to. If you notice it is not sticking completely, replace the sheet and continue to rub it until it's adhered. Repeat this step for all the letters.

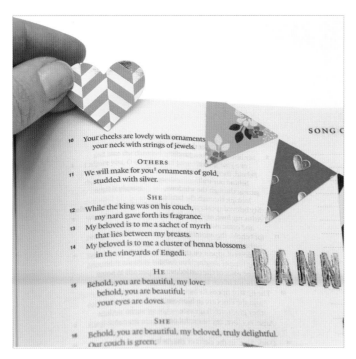

5 Adhere a heart sticker to the top of the page for a bookmark.

6 Flip the page over and adhere another same-size heart sticker over the first one. The two stickers should sandwich the page.

7 Use a black pen to draw strings at the ends of the banners.

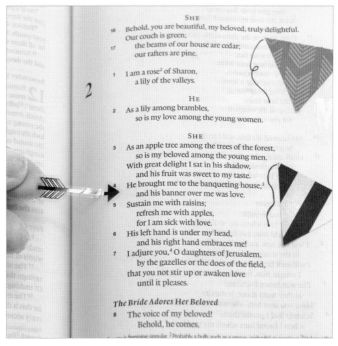

8 Adhere an arrow sticker to the page to point to the scripture passage.

Resources

Tools and Supplies

Altenew
altenew.com

American Crafts
americancrafts.com

Apollo
Available at office-supply stores and online.

Artist's Loft
michael's.com

Avery
avery.com

Caran d'Ache
store.carandache.com

ClearSnap
clearsnap.com

Cosmo Cricket
cosmocricket.com

Crafter's Workshop
store.thecrafters
workshop.com

Crayola
crayola.com

Dare 2B Artzy
dare2bartzy.com

DecoArt
decoart.com

Documented Faith
adornit.com

Doodlebug Design Inc.
doodlebug.ws

Echo Park Paper Co.
echoparkpaper.com

EK Success
Available at office-supply stores, craft stores, and online.

Faber-Castell
fabercastell.com

Fiskars
fiskars.com

Gelli Arts
gelliarts.com

The Girl's Paperie
emmaspaperie.com

Glue Dots
gluedots.com

Golden
goldenpaints.com

Heidi Swapp
heidiswap.com

Hero Arts
heroarts.com

Illustrated Faith
illustratedfaith.com

Kuretake
kuretakezig.us

Larkspur Hill
etsy.com/shop/larkspurhill

Lawn Fawn
lawnfawn.com

Lily Bee Design
emmaspaperie.com

Liquitex
liquitex.com/us

Marvy Uchida
uchida.com

May Arts
mayarts.com

Melt Art
rangerink.com

MT Tape
mt-tape.us

My Mind's Eye Paper Goods
mymindseye.com

My Sweet Petunia
mysweetpetunia.com

The Paper Studio
paperstudio.com

Papertrey Ink
papertreyink.com

Pentel Arts
pentel.com/pentel-arts

Pigma Micron
pigmamicron.com

Post-it
post-it.com

Prima Marketing Inc.
primamarketinginc.com

Prismacolor
prismacolor.com

Quick Quotes Scrapbook Company
shopquickquotes.com

Ranger
rangerink.com

Reeves
reeves-art.com

Sakura
sakuraofamerica.com

Scotch
scotchbrand.com

Sharpie
sharpie.com

Signo
uniball-na.com

Simple Stories
simplestories.com

Staedtler
staedtler.com/en

Stampendous!
stampendous.com

Stampers Anonymous
stampersanonymous.com

Stampin' Up!
stampinup.com

Stencil Girl
stencilgirlproducts.com

Studio Calico
studiocalico.com

Technique Tuesday
techniquetuesday.com

Tombow
tombowusa.com

Tsukineko
tsukineko.co.jp/english

Westcott
westcottbrand.com

WOW!
wowembossingpowder.com

Xyron
xyron.com

Zig
Distrubuted by Kuretake

Journaling Bibles

Crossway
crossway.org

Tyndale House Publishers
tyndale.com

Zondervan
zondervan.com

Index

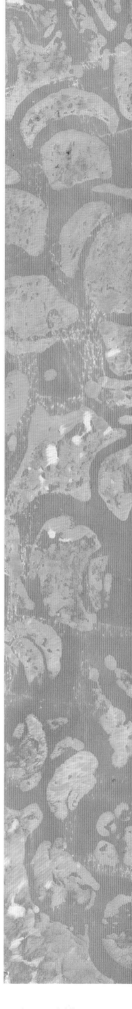

Bonus Art

The following pages include a wide variety of fun extras to use in your Bible art journaling, as well as templates and traceables featured in the projects.

Templates

Several of the projects incorporate shapes to be used as masks or to trace around. To use these templates, cut out the shapes with a sharp pair of scissors or craft knife on a craft mat. (You can also trace the templates or photocopy the page.) You can then use the templates as is or trace them onto a heavier card stock and cut them out. See the individual projects for specific instructions.

Traceable Art

I encourage you to draw and letter in your Bible freehand. The only way to improve is to practice as much as possible. However, if you would like to reproduce my lettering or artwork exactly, or if you need a jump-start in your own drawing and lettering, I have included traceable art for you to use. Place the art you would like to trace under the Bible page where you want it to appear, and place a light box under the art. It may be easier to trace certain areas if you cut them out of the larger sheet. You can also adhere the pieces directly to your Bible pages.

Vellum

In two of the projects in this book, I give instructions for painting and printing on deli papers. This allows you to create the patterns outside of your Bible and then glue it in when you're satisfied with it. I have included a sheet of vellum (transparent paper) printed with some of my designs. You can use it in several ways, including using the patterns as backgrounds on your Bible margins or cutting shapes out of them and adhering them to your page. To adhere them to your Bible page, brush a thin coat of gel medium on the back of the vellum paper with a sponge brush, place the vellum piece on the Bible page, then smooth it with your hands.

Stickers

We have included a variety of image stickers you can use to decorate your Bible pages or use as masks (for example, the "Seek" sticker is used as a mask in the Journaling over the Page project, page 88) and find tabs of all sixty-six books of the Bible. You'll also find stickers of faith-related words, which you you can use on your pages or place them on tabs to mark your Bible pages.

Die Cuts

We have also provided a sheet of punch-out die cuts, including tabs, tip-ins, and other decorative pieces. You can adhere them to your Bible pages with washi tape or adhesive. Feel free to further embellish them with words or art. The bookmark is used in a project (see Creating Embellishments on page 126).

Stencils (back flap)

The back flap of the book contains a handy ruler and a number of stencils you can use to trace images for your Bible page designs. There are stencils you can use to create additional tabs by tracing them onto card stock and cutting them out.

Crayons:
Two Ways
page 84

Gelatos
page 46

Creating Word Art
page 104

Doodling
page 38

Creating Letter Stickers
page 70

Stenciling with Watercolors
page 94

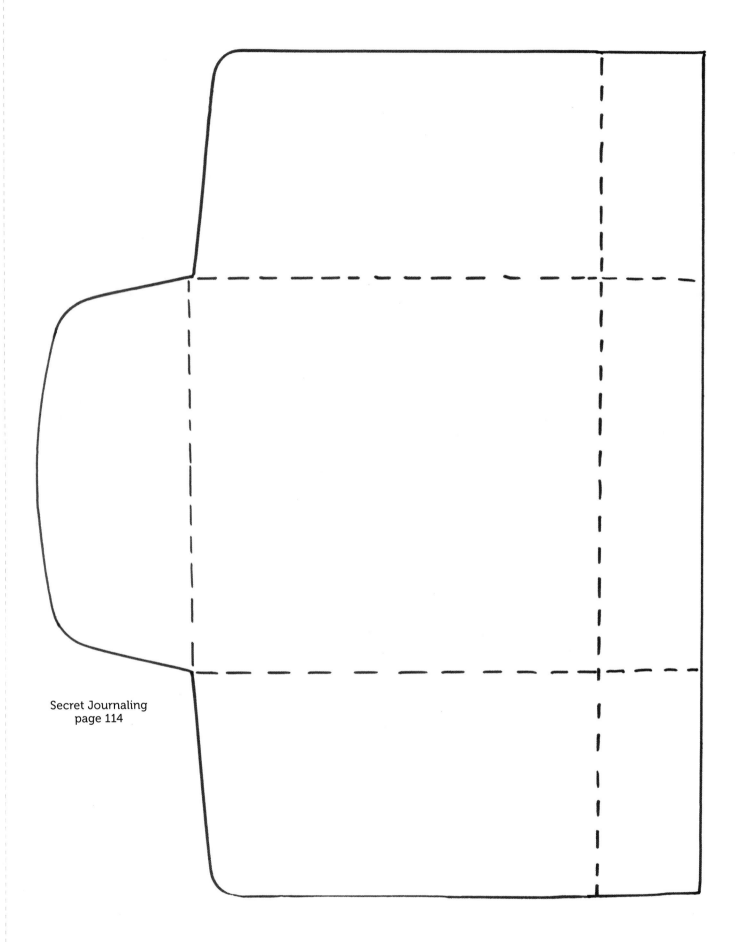

Secret Journaling
page 114

Creating Word Art
page 104

Traceable Word Art
page 74

Spray Inks
Page 62

the
trees
of the
forest
sing
for
joy
before
the
Lord

Creating Letter Stickers
page 70

LET YOUR
Faith
BE
BIGGER
your
THAN
fear

Secret Journaling
page 114

two
become
one

Photo Journaling
page 122

GOD
showers
COMPASSION
on His
creation
HIS faithful
followers:
will PRAISE
HIM &
Speak of the glory
of HIS
kingdom
HIS power, HIS
mighty deeds
& HIS majestic
reign

Creating Word Art
page 104

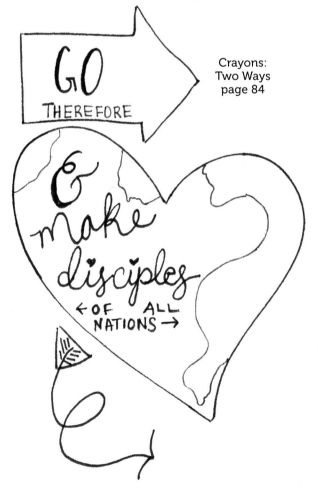

Crayons:
Two Ways
page 84

absolutely
NOTHING
can separate
Me FROM His
LOVE

Monoprinting
page 130

Just
do it!

Fearless Acrylic Painting
page 108

Hello

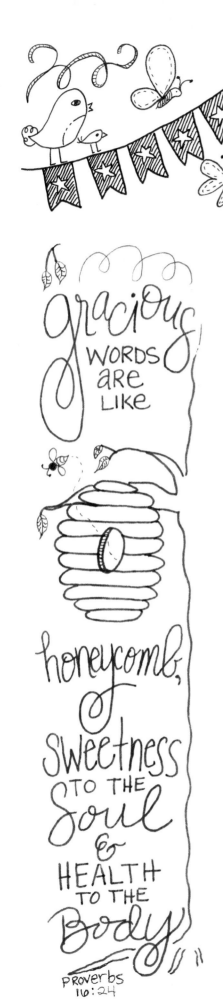

gracious WORDS ARE LIKE

honeycomb, sweetness TO THE Soul & HEALTH TO THE Body

Proverbs 16:24

TO Trust GOD in the light is NOTHING, BUT Trust HIM in the dark THAT is Faith

-Spurgeon

Speak

FOR THOSE WHO CANNOT SPEAK FOR THEMSELVES, FOR THE RIGHTS OF ALL WHO ARE DESTITUTE. SPEAK OUT FOR JUSTICE STAND UP FOR THE POOR AND NEEDY.

-PROV. 31:8-9

I Am the bread of life
Light of the World
the Gate
the Good Shepherd
the Resurrection & the LIFE
the Way and Truth and Life
THE true Vine

Let your faith be BIGGER Than your fear.

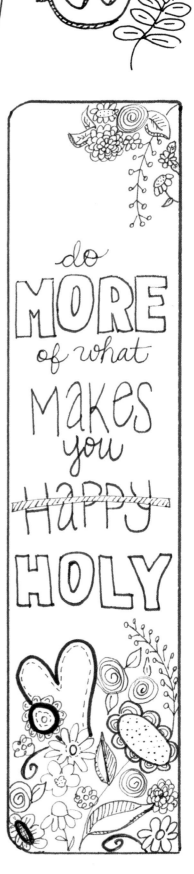

do MORE of what MAKES you HAPPY HOLY

My soul THIRSTS FOR you AS IN A dry & WEARY LAND.

— Psalms 63:1 —

my cup OVERFLOWS with Blessings

Blessed

Psalms 23:5

seek to do Good to one another

1 Thes. 5:15